a-Coffin Kuro by Satoko Kiyuduki

The traveler was waiting for the train she was to board.
To depart from here. To go to a new place.
She couldn't remember her destination.
But as long as she kept on traveling, she was a "traveler."

Characters
Shoulder-a-Coffin Kuro
Sen (A traveler who looks like a bat)
Kuro (A traveler with a coffin)
Sanju (An inexperienced traveler)
Nijuku (A novice traveler)

...CHAN.
KURO-CHAN?

IN A COUNTRY FARTHER NORTH THAN NORTH, THERE LIVED A BENEVOLENT FEUDAL LORD. UPON HIS PASSING...
...THE LAND WAS GIVEN TO HIS THREE SONS.

BUT THE ECCENTRIC MIDDLE SON...
...INHERITED ONLY THE DUSTY, OLD MANSION LOCATED IN THE FAR NORTHERN VILLAGE.

THE HEIR, THE ELDEST SON, INHERITED THE FORMER LORD'S AUTHORITY.
THE SINCERE AND KIND-HEARTED YOUNGEST SON INHERITED THE MOUNTAINS, PASTURES, AND LIVESTOCK.

I THINK WE'VE ARRIVED.
REMEMBER TO BE POLITE...
...AND GIVE YOUR BEST SMILE.

THIS IS A STORY ABOUT WHAT HAPPENED WITH THE ECCENTRIC MIDDLE SON INSIDE THE MANSION.

......HMM?

THE INTER-MEDIARY'S HERE, EH?

SHOULDER-A-COFFIN KURO

PLEASE WAIT. WHAT IS GOING ON!?
YOU'RE TELLING US TO LEAVE? WE JUST GOT HERE...

THE REASON'S OBVIOUS.
IT'S NOT WHAT I ASKED FOR.

I CHOSE ACCORDING TO YOUR REQUEST.
A CHILD WHO IS OVER SIX YEARS OLD, SMART...
...SENSIBLE, AND COULD BECOME A WORKER.

BUT I WANTED TO ADOPT A BOY.
THIS ONE'S A GIRL!

SHOO!
SHOO!
CAN'T YOU GET AROUND THAT LITTLE DETAIL?
SHE WAS REALLY HAPPY AT THIS CHANCE.
NO CAN DO. I CAN'T ADOPT UNLESS IT'S A BOY.

I'M SORRY, BUT TAKE HER AND LEAVE.

OH?
WHAT'S THAT?
WHISPER WHISPER

SHE'S SAYING IF YOU CAN'T ADOPT HER...
...AT WORST, SHE'S WILLING TO BECOME YOUR WIFE.
THAT FACE SAYS SHE'S TOTALLY AGAINST IT, DEEP DOWN!!

HOW ABOUT A WEEK? NO, EVEN THREE DAYS.
LET THE CHILD STAY WITH YOU.

SHE SEEMS TO LIKE YOU.
AND SURELY YOU CAN'T SAY YOU HAVEN'T STARTED TO FEEL FOR HER EITHER.

HEY, LET GO! WHAT ARE YOU—!?
CLATTER
STOP IT! I'M TELLING YOU TO STOP! YOU IDIOT!!
BANG

AND THEN THE LADY PUSHED THE CHILD THROUGH THE DOOR AND LEFT.
THAT'S WHY I HATE WOMEN.

WHAT ARE YOU DOING!!?
SWIPE
WHY ARE YOU SUDDENLY CUTTING YOUR HAIR!?

FINE. I'LL LET YOU STAY FOR ONE NIGHT.
CLATTER
CLACK
WHERE'S THE ORPHANAGE YOU CAME FROM?
I'LL CONTACT THEM, AND...

IF I LOOKED LIKE A BOY...
...IF I WASN'T A GIRL...
...I THOUGHT YOU WOULD LET ME STAY.

SWFFF
WHOA! UWAAH!

......
HEY, WHY DO YOU WANT TO STAY HERE SO BAD?
HAAAH...
...ANYWHERE'S FINE, AS LONG AS IT'S NOT THE ORPHANAGE.
THERE, I COULDN'T GET OUT.

I WANT TO HURRY UP AND TAKE CARE OF MYSELF, BE AN ADULT.
SO I CAN FIND MY MOTHER WHO LEFT TO GO WORK.

...OKAY, FINE.
I'LL LET YOU STAY, BUT THAT'S IT.
SCRITCH SCRITCH
!

OH, THANK... YOU.
MY NAME IS—
WHOA, DON'T TELL ME.
A NAME WILL MAKE ME AWARE OF YOUR "PRESENCE."

IN ORDER TO KEEP OUR RELATION-SHIP SIMPLE, I WON'T ASK YOUR NAME.
AND I WON'T TELL YOU MINE.
...... WHAT A WEIRD PERSON.

THEN WHAT SHOULD I CALL YOU?
I'D RATHER YOU DIDN'T...
...BUT I DON'T WANT YOU TO ADDRESS ME LIKE A CAT OR A TOY.
LIKE DADDY LONG-LEGS.

OKAY, YOU CAN CALL ME "SENSEI."
SENSEI?
THAT'S RIGHT. FOR A WHILE, I'LL BE YOUR TEACHER.

LISTEN, WE'RE STRANGERS UNTIL THE END.
ONCE YOU'RE READY TO LEAVE, GO AHEAD AND DO SO.
I'LL SEE YOU OFF HAPPILY.

IF YOU UNDER-STAND, GIVE ME YOUR BEST SMILE...
...AND A POLITE REPLY.
Y-YES, SENSEI!

AND SO, THE LITTLE GIRL WHO WENT IN AND OUT OF THE OLD MANSION...
...QUICKLY BECAME GOSSIP FOR THE VILLAGERS.

HEY, SENSEI! SENSEI!
HEY, DON'T BE SO FAMILIAR.
I JUST TOLD YOU YESTERDAY THAT WE'RE STRANGERS.

ALL KINDS OF PEOPLE ASKED ME ALL SORTS OF THINGS AS SOON AS I WENT OUT!
YOU HAVE A BIG REPUTATION.
AHHH, THEM.
I GUESS I DO...BUT JUST ONE DAY AND ALREADY THIS?

THEY SAY YOU'RE THE WEIRDEST, ODDEST ECCENTRIC, AND YOU BURY PEOPLE THAT COME NEAR HERE UNDER TREES.
AND YOU'RE WEAK AGAINST SUNLIGHT AND WILL TURN INTO ASHES, WHICH IS WHY YOU DON'T COME OUT.
AND WHAT'S WITH THE GARLIC AND THORNS!?
SO YOU'RE GOING TO BELIEVE STRANGERS YOU JUST MET OVER THE STRANGER LETTING YOU STAY!!?

MY FATHER WAS THE FEUDAL LORD WHO RULED THIS REGION FOR GENERATIONS.
UNLIKE MY EXEMPLARY OLDER BROTHER, I ABANDONED MY INHERITANCE AND CHOSE TO RETIRE IN QUIET...
...SO THE VILLAGERS TREAT ME LIKE AN ODDITY.

THAT'S WHY I WANTED TO ADOPT A KID WITHOUT A BACKGROUND WHO DIDN'T KNOW MY BAD REPUTATION.
I EVEN ASKED AN INTER-MEDIARY FROM AFAR.
BECAUSE THE PEOPLE AROUND HERE ONLY SEE ME AS A WEIRDO OR A MONSTER.
OHH.

I'M FINE WITH YOU.
AND I DON'T CARE WHAT KIND OF PERSON YOU MAY BE.
...... HMPH.

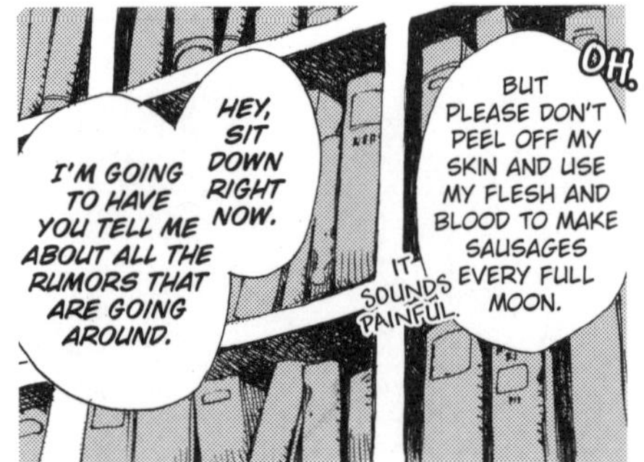
OH.
BUT PLEASE DON'T PEEL OFF MY SKIN AND USE MY FLESH AND BLOOD TO MAKE SAUSAGES EVERY FULL MOON.
IT SOUNDS PAINFUL.
HEY, SIT DOWN RIGHT NOW.
I'M GOING TO HAVE YOU TELL ME ABOUT ALL THE RUMORS THAT ARE GOING AROUND.

I'VE NOTICED LATELY THAT SHE'S BEEN ACTING STRANGELY EVERY SO OFTEN.
SNEAK
SHE TAKES THE BAG SHE CAME WITH AND SNEAKS AROUND THE MANSION.

......SO?
WHAT IS THIS?
......A SUN-DRESS.
IT'S... MINE.

IS SHE GETTING READY TO GO SO SOON?
WELL, THAT'S BETTER FOR ME ANYWAY.

IT WAS ONE OF THE DONATIONS AT THE ORPHAN-AGE.
I HAD TO FIGHT WITH THE OTHERS TO GET IT.
FOR SUCH A THIN PIECE OF CLOTH ...?

BUT IT'S SUSPICIOUS THAT SHE'S TRYING TO HIDE IT FROM ME.
IS SHE COLLECTING VALUABLES BEFORE SHE GOES?

BESIDES, THIS DRESS WON'T FIT YOU.
TH-THAT'S WHY...
...I KEEP CHECKING IF IT FITS ME FROM TIME TO TIME.

CLICK
EEEEP!?

BUT THE SUMMER IN THIS REGION IS REALLY SHORT.
I DON'T THINK YOU'LL HAVE MUCH CHANCE TO WEAR THIS ...
HEY!!
IT'S FINE!! I JUST WANTED IT, OKAY!!?
MEN DON'T UNDER-STAND!!

IT'S SUCH A PRETTY WHITE WITH A HINT OF LIGHT BLUE, SEE?
I LOVE THIS COLOR.
WHEN I WAS AT THE ORPHANAGE, I THOUGHT WHITE WAS A LITTLE MORE YELLOW.

THAT'S WHY I'M OKAY IF IT'S TOO BIG NOW.
'COS ONE DAY, IT'S GOING TO FIT ME PERFECTLY, RIGHT?

HEY, DO YOU THINK IT'LL LOOK GOOD ON ME THEN?
I DON'T KNOW. IT'S NOT GOING TO BE FOR A WHILE.

...... MAKE SURE TO CLEAN UP WHEN YOU'RE DONE.
I KNOW!
WHAT AM I SUPPOSED TO SAY...
...THAT WOULD BE CONSID-ERED THOUGHT-FUL?

BY THE WAY...
...YOU'RE ALWAYS READING, SENSEI.
HMM? YEAH...

YOU SHOULD READ TOO.
KNOWLEDGE IS THE SHORTCUT TO MATURING FASTER.
I CAN'T READ DIFFICULT WORDS.
SO IF THERE'S A BOOK WITH LOTS OF PICTURES, I'D GIVE IT A TRY.

WHAT KIND OF BOOK DO YOU WANT?
I'LL LOOK FOR SOMETHING.
UM...
...A BOOK ABOUT THE FOREIGN WORLD!!

A BOOK THAT HAS INFORMATION ABOUT COUNTRIES ALL OVER THE WORLD!
FINE, FINE.
AND A BOOK THAT TELLS YOU HOW TO GROW TALLER!
YOU NEED TO WORK ON THAT ON YOUR OWN.

HEY, LITTLE GIRL FROM THE OLD MANSION.
LOOKS LIKE THAT NUTCASE STILL HASN'T PICKLED YOU.
AH HA HA!

!
THUMP

OH.
I-I'M SORRY.

...HUH?

HEY.
I FOUND SOME BOOKS YOU MIGHT LIKE.

HM, SHE'S NOT HERE.
WHAT THE—? SHE'S ALREADY STARTED READING SOME.

HMM...? THEY'RE ALL FICTIONAL NOVELS.
AND THEY'RE FULL OF PICTURES.
SHE NEEDS TO READ MORE PRACTICAL BOOKS.

NOOOOOO!!
!?

NO! STOP IT!!
THIS IS... AWFUL!
WHOA, WHAT'S THIS?
HEY! WHAT'S GOING ON?
...... SEN-SEI?
NO. DON'T COME IN HERE!!
HUNH? WHAT DO YOU...
...MEAN?

COME BACK WHEN YOU...
...HAVE A BETTER PICKUP LINE.

......SEN...
...SEI.

HUH? WHICH ONE IS IT?
I CAN'T TELL IF YOU DON'T SPEAK.
...HUNH?

SENSEI?!

You feelin' better now?
YEAH.
SORRY I MADE YOU WORRY.
I think I was pretty beat too.
I had a weird dream 'cos of it.
A DREAM?
ABOUT WHAT?

...It's not worth telling.
OHH?

Hey, by the way...
...you used to have a thin white dress a long time ago, right?
HUH!? WHY ARE YOU ASKING ALL OF A SUDDEN?

HELLO. MAY I SIT HERE?
GO AHEAD.

I'M A TRAV-ELER.
SO NOWHERE IN PAR-TICULAR.

LET'S SEE...THE PLATFORM NORTH IS OVER THERE, I THINK?
WHERE ARE YOU HEADED?

IF I'M LUCKY TO GET ON A TRAIN...
...THAT'S WHERE I'M GOING.

OH DEAR, I'M SORRY I'M SUCH A COUNTRY BUMPKIN.
AND THIS IS MY FIRST EVER TRIP.
MY...

THIS IS MY FIRST TIME IN A PLACE AS BIG AS THIS.
MY, SUCH FREE-DOM. HOW NICE.

I WAS A TEACHER IN A SMALL VILLAGE FOR ABOUT FORTY YEARS.
MY KIDS GREW UP, AND MY WIFE PASSED AWAY, SO I HAD TOO MUCH TIME ON MY HANDS.
I SEE. THAT'S WHY YOU'RE ON A TRIP.

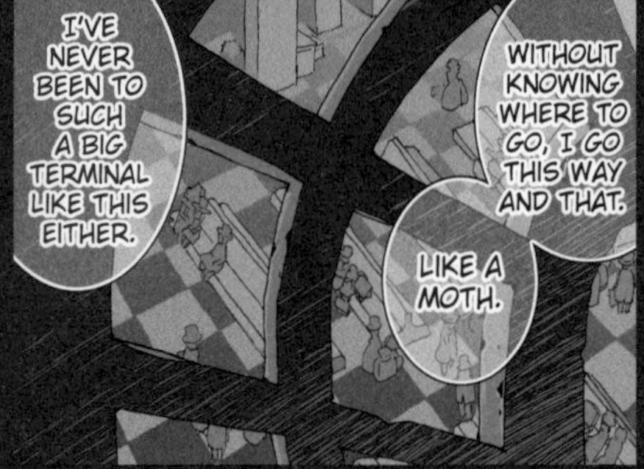
I'VE NEVER BEEN TO SUCH A BIG TERMINAL LIKE THIS EITHER.
WITHOUT KNOWING WHERE TO GO, I GO THIS WAY AND THAT.
LIKE A MOTH.

OH! YOU'RE A VETERAN TRAVELER.
A TEACHER, EH?
COULD YOU TEACH ME SOME-THING?

DEAR ME, LOOKING UP AT THIS HIGH A CEILING...
...IS SOMETHING I'VE ONLY EXPERIENCED IN THE BIGGEST CHURCH IN TOWN......

HOW IS ONE SUPPOSED TO ENJOY A JOURNEY?

...OR COULD IT REALLY BE A CHURCH ......?
OH!?
OH, THIS IS JUST MY LUG-GAGE.
PLEASE PAY IT NO MIND.

I'D ALWAYS WANTED TO GO VISIT DIFFERENT COUNTRIES, EVEN AS I GOT OLDER.
BUT NOW THAT I'M HERE, I GET SURPRISED AT THE BIG BUILDINGS AND TIRED FROM THE NOISE.
ALL THE UNFAMILIAR PEOPLE AROUND ME MAKE ME UNEASY.
...ARE YOU SAYING THAT I SHOULD BE MORE FREE?
NO, IT'S A LITTLE DIFFERENT.
EVERY TIME I FEEL UNCOMFORTABLE WHEREVER I GO...
...I FEEL LIKE I'M WASTING AN OPPORTUNITY.
WHAT CAN I DO TO ENJOY MY TRAVELS?
A TRAVELER IS AN EXISTENCE THAT ONLY PASSES THROUGH A PLACE, A SEASON.
SOMETIMES YOU'RE WELCOMED, LIKE THE SPRING WIND...
...OTHER TIMES DESPISED, LIKE THE COLD WIND OF WINTER.
....
HMM. WELL, I...
A TRAVELER IS JUST THAT BECAUSE HE DOESN'T BLEND IN WITH THAT SCENERY AND DOESN'T HAVE ANY EFFECT.
I DON'T THINK IT'S NECESSARY TO FEEL SOMETHING NOW.
I BELIEVE THAT A JOURNEY...
...IS LIKE BECOMING THE WIND.
ONCE YOU'VE TRAVELED THE WORLD...
...IT MIGHT BE WHEN YOU START A FIRE IN YOUR FIREPLACE AT HOME...
...THAT YOU'LL HAVE YOUR ANSWER.

OH NO! WHAT SHOULD I DO?
THIS IS MOST UNBE-COMING.

GOODNESS, THE THINGS YOU SAY ARE LIKE POEMS.
I CAN ONLY BE VAGUE.
IT'S THE NATURE OF A TRAV-ELER.

...IS SOME-THING THE MATTER?
MY RIBBON CAME UNDONE.
SO MUCH FOR HAVING A CHIC DRESS!

AH, I SHOULD GO.
PLEASE TAKE THIS, FELLOW TRAVELER.

HEY, COULD YOU PERHAPS FIX IT FOR ME?
HUH?
...BUT I DON'T KNOW WHAT IT'S SUPPOSED TO LOOK LIKE.
DON'T WORRY. LOOK TO YOUR RIGHT.

? ARE YOU SURE?
I BOUGHT TOO MANY FROM AN ENTHU-SIASTIC PEDDLER.

THERE'S YOUR "EXAMPLE."
EH!?

BUT I HOPE THAT I CAN REMEMBER MEETING YOU...
...EVERY TIME I HAVE AN ORANGE.

I SEE. YOU'RE SISTERS.
YES.
TWINS, TO BE EXACT.
OH? IS SOMETHING THE MATTER?
OH! NO.
I JUST REMEMBERED I KNEW ANOTHER PAIR OF TWINS...
SISTER, IS THAT SOME NEW KIND OF FLIRTING?
MY.
YOU TWO MUST GET ALONG TO BE TRAVELING TOGETHER. HOW NICE.
YES, WE GET ALONG VERY WELL.
BUT THIS IS OUR LAST DAY TOGETHER.
I'M GOING WEST TO WORK. MY LITTLE SISTER WILL GO EAST FOR COLLEGE.
WE EACH HAVE A DIFFERENT TICKET.
WE'RE DISEMBARKING AT DIFFERENT LOCATIONS.
WE'VE ALWAYS BEEN TOGETHER...
...GOING TO THE SAME PLACES, DOING THE SAME THINGS.
NO, WE WERE "US" BECAUSE WE WERE TOGETHER.
WE'VE NEVER IMAGINED LIFE WITHOUT THE OTHER.
WE'RE GOING TO BE SEPARATED FOR THE FIRST TIME.
IT FEELS LIKE A RAZOR SLICING...
...OUR JOINED FINGERTIPS APART.
DO YOU THINK...
...WE'LL EACH BE FINE ON OUR OWN?

...DO YOU LIKE ORANGES?
HOW LOVELY!
WHAT A BIG ORANGE.
......IT SMELLS GOOD.
YES, IT'S STILL FRESH.
THEY BOTH SMELL THE SAME.
IF YOU DON'T CUT IT...
...THIS ORANGE WOULD STAY AN ORANGE TILL THE END OF ITS DAYS.
PERHAPS IT WOULD BE HAPPY THAT WAY.
I'LL BECOME A DELICIOUS MARMALADE.
BUT IF YOU DO CUT IT...
...NEW OPPORTUNITIES WILL PRESENT THEMSELVES.
AND I'LL BECOME A FINE ORANGE SAUCE TO GO WITH DUCK.
IT'S UP TO EACH OF YOU...
...HOW TO EAT IT.
OH! BUT THE SKIN OF YOUR ORANGE IS MUCH TOO THICK!!
AND YOURS HAS TOO MANY SEEDS INSIDE!
BICKER
BICKER
THEY'RE BOTH THE SAME.

THANK YOU. I WISH WE COULD REPAY YOU FOR THE ORANGE SOMEHOW...
I KNOW! TAKE THIS!

I'LL LET YOU KNOW WHEN THE TRAIN COMES.
IT WAS A DOLL ...?
THANK YOU.
MY RIGHT EYE WAS STARTING TO GET BLURRY TOO, AND I WAS AT A LOSS.

I JUST BROUGHT IT WITH ME FROM HOME BECAUSE I WAS LONELY.
BUT I NEED TO GROW UP!
...... THANK YOU...

SEEING AS YOU DO, SURELY YOU'RE NOT GOING TO A BATTLE-FIELD?
NO, SADLY...
...I'VE BECOME USELESS, SO I'M HEADING HOME.

ER...
EXCUSE ME, MAY I ASK...

OH, THE TRAIN'S HERE ALREADY.
YOU WERE HEADING SOUTH...

...WHICH TRAIN IS GOING SOUTH?
....

...RIGHT ......?
HUH?

....
I BELIEVE THAT PEOPLE REMEMBER THEIR HOMES IN THEIR BONES...
...THE SAME AS BIRDS AND FISH, AND WILL GO BACK HOME NO MATTER WHAT.
...YOU DON'T WANT TO GO HOME?
NO, I DO.
BUT I'M SCARED.
BUT WITH HUMANS, WE ALWAYS CHOOSE TO BE COMPLICATED FOR SOME REASON.
WE MIGHT GO HOME IN THREE DAYS...
...OR WE MIGHT GO BACK IN SIXTY YEARS.
THE PLACE I GREW UP IS STRICT AND MILITARISTIC.
MY FRIENDS AND I ALL SIGNED UP FOR THE ARMY AND LEFT HOME WILLINGLY.
THREE DAYS OR SIXTY YEARS—
IT'S YOUR CHOICE AS LONG AS YOU DON'T REGRET IT.
MY MOTHER WOULD BE SAD TO SEE ME LIKE THIS.
AND MY PATRIOTIC FATHER MIGHT BE ASHAMED.
BUT IF THERE'S SOMEONE WAITING FOR YOUR RETURN...
...I THINK THAT'S REASON ENOUGH.
THE BATTLEFIELD REJECTED ME ALREADY. PERHAPS THE SAME WILL HAPPEN IN MY HOME-TOWN.
EVEN SO, IS IT OKAY FOR ME TO GO BACK?

...THIS DOLL REMINDS ME OF MY CHILDHOOD FRIEND.
SHE HAD BEAUTIFUL HAIR.
OHH?
STEAM
STEAM
THEN PLEASE TAKE IT AS YOUR TRAVEL COMPANION.
WHAT!?
...WELL, I SUPPOSE YOU'RE RIGHT. IT MIGHT BE PERFECT BECAUSE I'M SUCH A COWARD.
...OH NO!
I DON'T BELIEVE THIS!
OH! THEN PLEASE TAKE THIS IN RETURN. IT'S A CHARM FROM MY HOMETOWN TO KEEP ME SAFE...
A CHARM?
IT WILL PROTECT YOU ON YOUR TRAVELS.
UM, HAVE YOU SEEN THE THIN YOUNG MAN WITH THE INJURED EYE?
HE... WAS MY CHILDHOOD FRIEND...
OHH, HE JUST LEFT ON THAT TRAIN.
IT WORKS! I SWEAR!
...I CAN SEE THAT IT HAS ALREADY WORKED ONCE FOR YOU.
JANGLE
......!
NO...
...BUT I THOUGHT HIS EYES HAD JUST HEALED...

...YOU CAN HAVE THESE FLOWERS.
BECAUSE I COULDN'T GIVE THEM TO HIM.
AH.
MY TRAIN'S FINALLY HERE.
HE SAID HE WAS GOING HOME.
IF YOU'RE HIS CHILDHOOD FRIEND, WON'T YOU SEE HIM AGAIN?
THIS WAS OUR LAST GOOD-BYE.
SO NO, I WON'T SEE HIM AGAIN.
...HUH?
EVER.

MY LUGGAGE ...
...AND CLOTHES?
DARN! I NEED TO GO GET THEM.

I CAN'T REMEMBER.
WHAT WAS I LOOKING FOR?

HOW WEIRD. WHY DID I LEAVE THEM THERE?
I CAN'T CONTINUE ON MY WAY WITHOUT THEM.

RRRRING
THERE'S THE DEPARTURE BELL!

...HUH?
WAIT, HOLD ON.

THE REASON...
...I'M TRAVELING IS...

WHY AM I...
... TRAVELING AGAIN?

...I'M......

STEAM
STEAM

WELL, IT'S FINE.
I'M USED TO NOT HAVING THINGS GO MY WAY.

HELLO!
WHERE ARE YOU HEADED?

....
I COULDN'T GET ON *AGAIN.*

I'M A TRAVELER.
SO NOWHERE IN PAR-TICULAR.

WHEN WILL I BE ABLE TO...
...LEAVE THIS TERMINAL?

IF I'M LUCKY TO GET ON A TRAIN...
...THAT'S WHERE I'M GOING.

Shoulder-a-Coffin Kuro by Satoko Kiyuduki

She was going to see a friend she'd met again a year ago.
She was going to see that friend once more.
To a snowy place that wasn't on any map,
the good friend "walked" on.

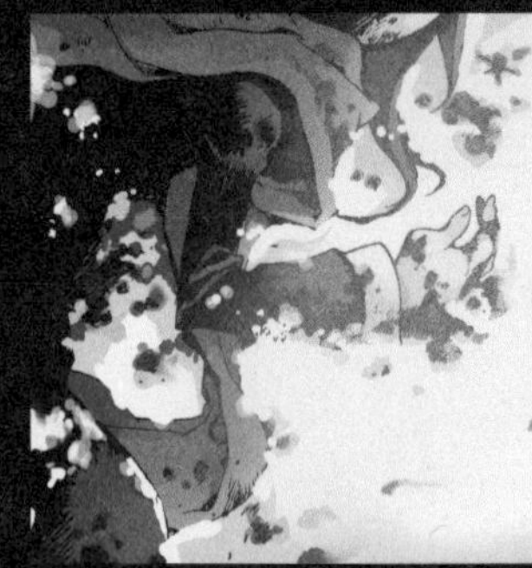
EVER SINCE KURO-CHAN TURNED BLACK AND WENT TO SLEEP...

...THE WORLD TURNED GREEN...
...THE BROWN THINGS FELL...

...EVEN WHEN THE WHITE THING MELTED...
...YELLOW THINGS GREW...

...AND THE WHITE THING CAME BACK...

...EVEN THEN, KURO-CHAN DIDN'T WAKE UP.

IS IT "NO" TODAY TOO?
STILL, "NO."
SEN SAID WE CAN'T COME IN.
NIJUKU, DO YOU REMEMBER PROFES-SOR?
OF COURSE!
I WOULD NEVER FORGET PROFES-SOR!
BORING.
IF WE CAN'T EVER SEE HER...
...WE'LL FORGET KURO-CHAN.
HIS GREAT, BIG BODY.
AND HIS WARM, ROUGH HANDS.
?
WHAT DOES IT MEAN TO "FORGET"?
UM...
...THE OPPOSITE OF REMEM-BER.
...HUH?
THE *TOP* OF PROFESSOR ISN'T COMING TO ME.
WHAT WE KNEW, WE WON'T KNOW ANYMORE.
AND WHAT WE DIDN'T KNOW, WE WON'T KNOW EITHER.
IT'S WHITE AND FUZZY, BUT...
...I DON'T KNOW WHY I CAN'T SEE HIS FACE.
YEAH.
ME TOO.

ARE WE GOING TO "FORGET" KURO-CHA LIKE THAT TOO?
DON'T WORRY. I HAVE A PLAN.
WE SHOULD PLAY "TRAVELER"...
...SO WE WON'T FORGET KURO-CHAN!
"TRAV-ELER?"
WE REMEMBER WHAT KURO-CHAN DID WHILE WE TRAVELED...
...AND COPY HER!
THEN WE WON'T FORGET KURO-CHA!
YEAH! LET'S DO IT!
AND KURO-CHAN WILL BE—
ばっ
WHIP
ME!
ばっ
WHIP
PHEWWW! IT'S SO COLD.
HEY, SANJU.
YOU PLAYING ALONE TODAY?
CLOP
I'M NOT...
...SANJU.
......?
CRUNCH
CRUNCH

JUST TO LET YOU KNOW, I DIDN'T LOSE.
I LET YOU HAVE IT 'COS I'M THE BIG SISTER.
YEAH, YEAH. I GOT IT, "SEN."
FLAP ぱた
FLAP ぱた
OKAY, SEN, LET'S GO.
SURE.
KURO, YOU DIDN'T FORGET ANYTHING, RIGHT?
ぱた FLAP
YEAH. I HAVE MY STUFF.
FLAP ぱた
I HAVE MY HAT.
WHAT'S LEFT IS...
OH!
NIJUKU AND SANJU AREN'T HERE!
OH!
YOU'RE RIGHT! WHERE'D THEY GO?
TRAVELERS? THERE ARE A LOT GOING BY AROUND HERE.
OH.
UM, THE ONE I'M LOOKING FOR...
...IS DRESSED IN BLACK AND CARRIES A COFFIN...
KURO, YOU LOOK OVER THERE!
I'LL GO SEARCH THAT WAY.
HUH?
OH!
THERE YOU ARE! IT'S BEEN A WHILE, YOU TWO.
CRUNCH ザッ
DO YOU REMEMBER ME?
CRUNCH ザッ
HEYYY, KURO! I FOUND 'EM!
NIJUKU AND SANJU!
SAY WHAT?

OH, YOU'RE JUST PLAYING.
I'M KURO-CHAN.
I'M SEN.
OKAY, SO LET'S GO, SANJU! NIJUKU!
HUH?
WHERE ARE WE GOING?
ISN'T IT OBVI-OUS?
WE'RE GONNA TRAVE—
WHUMP
...SHOULD I SAVE YOU?
"KURO-CHAN"?
YES, PLEASE.
AREN'T YOU SUPPOSED TO BE A BAT?
HEY, LITTLE ONES.
PLAYING A NEW GAME?
WE'RE TRAVELERS ON A JOURNEY.
HOH! IS THAT RIGHT?
BE CAREFUL OUT THERE.
DO YOU KNOW A PLACE THAT WOULD TREAT US WANDERERS NICE?
ROUND HERE? JUST THIS COMMUNITY.
GO MAKE A ROUND AND THEN COME BACK.
THANKS, GRAMPS.
ALSO, IF YOU COULD TELL ME WHERE TO FIND THE BEAUTIFUL GIRLS......
DRAG
DRAG
DRAG
SEN!
KIDS REALLY WATCH WHAT WE DO, DON'T THEY...?

LOOK! A RIVER.
LET'S HOP ON THE STONES TO GET ACROSS.
THE ONE WITH THE LIGHTEST *BODY* SHOULD GO FIRST.
I SEE.
THAT MAKES SENSE.
THEN SEN FIRST...
...AND THEN YOU, SANJU.
HUH!? OH, I'M SANJU, HUH?
NO WAY. I'M PROBABLY THE HEAVIEST IN THIS BUNCH...
SANJU ISN'T THAT HEAVY!
FINE, FINE!
DASH
IT'S ALL SO CONFUSING! GEEZ!
LET'S TAKE A BREAK HERE.
WHAT!? WE ONLY CROSSED A LITTLE RIVER.
WHAT A SLOW JOURNEY...
I'M TIRED OF CARRYING THIS.
AND I'M TIRED OF FLYING.
THESE KIDS...
OH, ALL RIGHT.
SHALL I CARRY IT FOR YOU?
NO.
I'M COPYING KURO-CHAN.
KURO-CHAN CARRIED IT ALL BY HERSELF...
...THE WHOLE TIME.

HM? HEY, WAIT!
WHAT'S WRONG WITH YOUR SHOES?
ARE YOU SURE YOU CAN WALK IN THOSE?
USUALLY KURO-CHA FIXED THEM FOR ME.
IF YOU LEAVE THEM ALONE FOR A YEAR, OF COURSE THEY'LL BREAK.
KURO-CHAN ALSO MADE THE EARS FOR OUR HATS!
I GUESS A TRAVELER HAS TO BE ABLE TO DO MANY THINGS.
GO SEE THE OLD MAN AT THE STABLES LATER.
BUT FOR SOME REASON, JUST THAT DAY...
...KURO-CHAN DIDN'T WANNA HOLD HANDS.
DOESN'T IT SEEM LIKE WE'RE GOING DEEPER INTO THE WOODS?
ARE WE GOING TO BE ABLE TO GET BACK?
NO WORRIES. WE HAVEN'T COME IN TOO FAR.
WHEN WE'RE LOST, WE USE THIS, RIGHT?
WHAP
A "MAP!"
KURO-CHAN, WHAT'S THAT?
OH.
THIS IS A MAP.
WE KNOW "HALF" OF...
...WHAT LIES AHEAD OF US WHEN WE USE THIS.

KURO-CHAN LOOKED AT THE "MAP"...
...BUT SHE WAS LOOKING FAR AWAY TOO.
WE CAN'T GO ANY FARTHER.
SO THIS IS THE END OF OUR JOURNEY.
......THE END?
FAR PAST THE "MAP."
FAR PAST THE ROAD.
FAR PAST THE SKY.
A JOURNEY ENDS?
OF COURSE.
EVERY-THING ENDS EVENTU-ALLY.
SHE WAS LOOKING FAR, FAR AWAY.
I'LL BET SHE WAS LOOKING AT...
...WHAT WAS IN THE REST OF THE "HALF."
....
WHAT'S WRONG?
YOU WANT TO PLAY MORE?
THE THING SHE WAS SEEKING OUT...
...ON HER TRAVELS.
WE THOUGHT IT WOULD ALWAYS BE LIKE THIS.
SO WE NEVER THOUGHT ABOUT THAT.

WHAT HAPPENS WHEN A JOURNEY ENDS?
WHAT HAPPENS TO US AND KURO-CHAN?
...WE CAN'T ANSWER THAT.
WHEN SHE WAKES UP, SHE'LL TELL YOU.
SO UNTIL THEN, WE HAVE TO WAIT.
...'KAY!
WE'LL WAIT NO MATTER HOW MANY TIMES THIS *WHITE THING* COMES!
...I HOPE SHE WAKES UP BEFORE WE'RE ALL OLD.
WELL, I'D BETTER GET GOING.
OH! ME TOO.
I WAS ASKED TO SHARPEN THE FARMING TOOLS!
GOOD-BYE, LITTLE TRAVELERS.
TAKE CARE ON YOUR JOURNEY.
ARE YOU "TRAVELING" TOO?
I NEED TO SEE YOUR COMPANION.
I'VE BEEN LOOKING ALL OVER.
OH.
THEY'RE IN THE WOOD CABIN.
Y'KNOW, THE CRUMBLING ONE NEAR WHERE WE MET.
HURRY UP AND TAKE ME THERE!!
THAT WAS A BIG WASTE OF TIME!!
CRUNCH
CRUNCH
CRUNCH
TAKE CARE ON YOUR JOURNEY!

WE DIDN'T FORGET AFTER ALL.
YEAH.
WE DIDN'T FORGET KURO-CHAN.
PHEW, I MADE IT...
BAT-KUN, ARE YOU HEEERE?
...BUT THERE'S ONE THING THAT I COULDN'T REMEMBER.
YEAH.
I COULDN'T REMEMBER ONE THING TOO.
HUNH?
It's you, Chou!
KURO-CHA'S FACE.
Oh, it's been a year already, eh?
HOW IS SHE DOING?
A BLACK, FOGGY THING IS IN THE WAY...
...AND I CAN'T REMEMBER WHAT KURO-CHA'S FACE LOOKED LIKE.
Well, as you can see...
...she's hanging in there, thanks to you.

SHE SAID SHE'S A "TRAVELER," SO I BROUGHT HER HERE.
SHE'S LUCKY TO HAVE ALMOST DIED IN FRONT OF A HIDE-AWAY.
HA HA HA!
IS THAT YOUR KID?
NO WAY.
I PICKED HER UP 'COS SHE WAS AT DEATH'S DOOR.
YOU ON THE WAY TO GRANDMA'S OR SOME-THING?
YOU SHOULD GO HOME BEFORE A WOLF EATS YOU.
BUT I CAN ONLY GO FORWARD.
IN THE DIRECTION I CAN SEE BEFORE ME.
YOU DON'T HAVE TO TELL ME.
I ALREADY KNOW.
......
I WONDER IF I STILL HAVE IT.
HERE WE GO.
I'LL GIVE YOU THIS.
A ROCK ...?
NO, AN OLD COIN?
REMEMBER THIS.
WHEN THINGS GET REALLY BAD...
...LOOK FOR THE "TOROKUSHI GATHER-ING."

CHOU, THERE'S NO MISTAKE.
ACCORDING TO THAT TRAVELER, THE SIMOUN WAS FOUND CRASHED AT THE SITE OF THAT BLACK SMOKE.

I THOUGHT YOU WERE MY FRIEND. BUT YOU SHOWED UP WITH A COFFIN ON YOUR BACK, SO...
ARE YOU SURE YOU'RE NOT DEATH HIM-SELF!?
...NO!! I WON'T BE-LIEVE IT!!
ARE YOU SURE YOU SAW GRAND-PA!?
......
SORRY...
!? YOUR... FACE!!
HEY, WHAT'S GOING ON!? WAIT!!

OH! SHE'S RECOVERED QUITE NICELY. SHE LOOKS BETTER THAN I EXPECTED.
Yeah. The "attack" has completely subsided.
BUT...SHE WENT BACK TO NORMAL AFTER TWO OR THREE DAYS, THEN, RIGHT?
Yeah, she's never had one this bad.
If you hadn't delivered them, I don't know if she would have survived.
...IT REMINDED ME OF WHEN MY GRANDFATHER DIED.
IT'S THE SAME THING AS THEN, RIGHT?
Yeah, "that."
It hasn't happened since, so it caught me totally off guard.
By the way, were you able to go to the witch's house again?
OHHH.
ACTUALLY, I COULDN'T FIND IT, NO MATTER HOW HARD I LOOKED.
IT'S SUCH A MYSTERY.
When she was younger, she had more of "these."
It was especially worse on days when she encountered death.
When her negative emotions run high, it comes out.
......YOU SAW...
...THE WITCH...?
LIKE I SAID, I COULDN'T ...
Once she figured out how to distance herself and kill her emotions...
...it stopped almost entirely.
What you said back then, words from someone her own age, must've gotten to her.
!?
WHIP

YOU'RE AWAKE, BLACK TRAV-ELER !?
DO YOU... KNOW WHO I AM?

...OH?
CHOU...

....

......DID I DIE?
UNFOR-TUNATELY, WE'RE NOT IN THE HEAVENS.

HI, SEN.
Hey, it's been a while.

OH, SO I HAD AN "ATTACK."
...I FEEL LIKE I WAS HAVING A LONG DREAM.
I see.
I feel like I just finished a long prison sentence.

CHOU, CAN YOU HOLD ONTO SEN'S WING FOR ME?
HUH? OH, SURE.
WHAT FOR? TO THANK HIM?
?

NO, TO CAPTURE HIM BEFORE HE TAKES OFF.
HE TENDS TO HIT THE BOTTLE AFTER NURSING SOMEONE BACK TO HEALTH OR DOING SOMETHING UNFAMILIAR AND DOESN'T COME BACK FOR AGES.
FLAP
FLAP
FLAP
FLAP
FLAP
FLAP
WHOA!

OH, WHERE ARE MY GLASSES ...?
WHOA!?
HEY, HOLD ON A SEC-OND!!
WHY ARE YOU NAKED!!?
WHERE ARE YOUR CLOTHES !?
THEY'D JUST GET DIRTY ANYWAY.
Well, it was a Hassle to change Her every time, so...
KNOCK
KNOCK
HEY, I GOT SOME HOT WATER.
KYAAAH!! NO!! DON'T COME IN!!
ALL MALES NEED TO GET OUUUT—!!
So you're letting me go anyway!!
Whoa, it's cold out Here!!
I'LL WRAP YOU UP WITH BANDAGES, SO COME HERE.
THANKS.
BY THE WAY, WHY ARE YOU HERE?
SEE THOSE HERBS ON THE TABLE?
I DELIVERED THEM 'COS A LADY I MET ON A HILL ASKED ME TO.
BUT YOU WERE IN REALLY BAD SHAPE ...
...AND THE AMOUNT I BROUGHT WASN'T ENOUGH.
SO BAT-KUN COLLECTED THE SEEDS ...
...AND GREW THE HERBS FOR THE PAST YEAR.
AND HE USED THEM, BIT BY BIT, TO MAKE YOU BETTER.

AS SOON AS HE USED THE HERBS, YOU HEALED QUICKLY.
SO HE SAID IT WAS WORTH THE WAIT.
...I SEE.
HE TRULY CARES ABOUT YOU.
YUCK.
STOP ASSUMING WEIRD THINGS.
HE'S ACTUALLY A HUMAN, RIGHT?
WE'RE ONLY TRAVELING TOGETHER BECAUSE WE HAVE A COMMON GOAL.
I KNOW.
YOU TWO WERE CURSED BY AN EVIL WITCH.
AND YOU'RE TRAVELING TOGETHER TO RETURN TO YOUR ORIGINAL FORMS.
YOU'RE ON A QUEST TO FIND A PRINCESS WHO'LL KISS HIM, RIGHT?
THAT'S JUST THE STORY HE USES TO PICK UP WOMEN.
OKAY, ALL DONE.
DOES IT HURT ANY-WHERE?
...I DON'T THINK THEY'RE TIGHT ENOUGH.
YOU DO THEM UP TOO TIGHT!
YOU WERE ALWAYS COVERED IN BANDAGE MARKS.
OKAY, YOU GUYS CAN COME IN NOW.
OH? WHERE'S BAT-KUN?
BOB
PHEW, I THOUGHT I'D FREEZE TO DEATH.

OH!
YOUR FRIEND FINALLY WOKE UP!
Kuro.
What's the last thing you remember before you fell uncon-scious?
HELLO.
THANKS FOR LETTING US STAY.
YOU DON'T NEED TO THANK ME.
YOU SHOULD GO SEE NIJUKU AND SANJU INSTEAD.
....
WHAT'S KURO?
Okay, I get it. Never mind.
THEY SHOWED UP AT THE CABIN EVERY DAY TO SEE HOW YOU WERE.
YEAH.
THEY'RE GOING TO BE SO THRILLED TO FINALLY SEE YOU.
YOU'RE HAPPY TOO, RIGHT ...?
OH? DID SHE LOSE HER MEMO-RY?
BUT SHE REMEM-BERS ME.
Part of her memory seems to be missing.
...OH?
DID THEY NOT...
...GET ALONG?
Actually, I didn't expect this reaction.
Well, she did experience the bitterest good-bye of her life.
I can understand if her body's defenses blocked the memory.

MAYBE IT'LL COME BACK IF YOU HIT HER A FEW TIMES.
HER MEMORY, I MEAN ...
Don't treat her like you treat your junky plane.
Actually, there's no point in making her remember.
BUT SHE'S FORGOTTEN ABOUT THE LITTLE ONES TOO.
Perhaps it's for the best.
She can get to know them from the beginning again.
It's not a hard thing to do.
...YEAH, EVERYTHING WILL BE BACK TO NORMAL IN NO TIME!
RIGHT, BLACK TRAV-ELER ...?
Hm?
Where'd Kuro go?
...IT'S COLD.
MY LUNGS HURT.
...IN THE END...
...I COULDN'T GET ON THE TRAIN...

...HM?
CHIL-DREN'S VOICES ...?
AH HA HA HA!
KYAAAAH!

I FOUND NEW FOOT-PRINTS!
NIJUKU, OVER HERE!!

THEY'RE FROM SOMEONE BIGGER THAN US.
WHO COULD THESE BELONG TOOO?

IT WAS MISTER RABBIT.
HE'S SMALLER THAN US.
IT'S COLD.

...WHAT AM I DOING ...?
I DIDN'T HAVE TO HIDE FROM SOME KIDS...

BUT... WHAT IS THIS?
THERE'S AN UNEASE IN MY CHEST, AND IT DOESN'T FEEL GOOD.

I DON'T KNOW WHY...
...BUT I DON'T WANT TO GO NEAR THEM.

WE TOLD YOU OUR NAMES!
YOUR TURN NOW!

WHO IN THE WORLD ARE YOU?

PITCH-BLACK BLACK...
...BLACK PERSON-SAN.

....
LET'S SEE.

WELL, SINCE I'M IN ALL BLACK...
...THAT MAKES ME... KURO THE TRAVELER?

I DON'T REALLY KNOW WHY...
...BUT I DON'T WANT TO GO NEAR THEM.

MINE'S BIGGER, RIGHT?
NO, MINE IS!

I SHOULD GO BACK TO THE CABIN...
...BEFORE THEY SEE ME.

SEE, MINE'S BIGGER!
NO WAY! MINE IS!
ROLL ROLL RO

FLINCH

IT WON'T MOVE ANYMORE?
NO, IT WON'T MOVE.
AGAIN!!?
FLINCH

FLINCH
THEN LET'S STOP.
LET'S PLAY SOMETHING ELSE.

HFF!
HFF!

WHAT SHOULD WE DO NEXT?
HM, HMM! LET'S SEE!

SHEESH ...
HFF!
USUALLY, THEY'RE NOWHERE TO BE FOUND WHEN I'M LOOKING FOR THEM.
HFF!
HFF!
...WAIT, WHAT WAS THAT ...?
WHAT AM I SAYING ...?
ドドド
RUMBLE RUMBLE
HM?
WHAT'S THAT SOUND?
AH, that's snow.
I'll bet they're shaking down the snow from the roof or trees for fun.
THERE, SEE! I DROPPED MORE SNOW!
I WIN, NIJUKU!
URGH!
THEN I'LL DROP ALL OF THE WHITE STUFF HERE!
HEY, NOT FAIR!!
TAKE THAT! AND THAT!!
KICK
KICK
I'M GONNA DO THAT TOO!
...HUH?
WHAT'S THIS BLACK THING?

THAT BLACK HAND IS NO GOOD.
DON'T TOUCH IT.

STAY AWAY.
STAY AWAY.
STAY AWAY.

STOP!
DON'T TOUCH ME!!

...OH.

S— SORRY.
UM... DID YOU WANT ME TO CALL YOUR COMPANIONS?
NO, IT'S FINE. I'M SORRY.
I WAS JUST DREAMING.

THAT'S RIGHT. YOU WERE ILL, WEREN'T YOU?
YOU SHOULDN'T BE WALKING AROUND UNTIL YOU COLLAPSE.

AND YOU WERE SO LIGHT WHEN I CARRIED YOU HERE.
I WAS SURPRISED.
THAT'S RIGHT. YOU NEED TO REGAIN YOUR STRENGTH.

WHEN SPRING COMES, THERE'S PLOWING AND SOWING TO BE DONE.
...AM I NOT ALLOWED TO LEAVE BEFORE THEN?

AH! HA-HA! I'M KIDDING.
BUT... YOU'VE BEEN HERE FOR SO LONG, I THOUGHT YOU MIGHT END UP "STAYING," LIKE US.
LIKE YOU ...?
WE USED TO TRAVEL ALL OVER THE WORLD TOO.
MY LITTLE BROTHER DOESN'T REMEMBER MUCH OF IT.
OHHH ...
WE WERE PART OF A TRAVELLING COMPANY OF ENTERTAINERS.
I WAS PRETTY SKILLED IN WHAT I DID.
AH, LET ME GUESS.
THROWING KNIVES?
THAT'S RIGHT.
THIS MAN IN THE PICTURE IS...
MY BELOVED HUSBAND.
HE WAS ALSO PART OF THE COMPANY.
HE'S AN ILLUSIONIST.
HE USUALLY COMES HOME WHEN THE PICTURE GETS TOO TATTERED.
WITH A NEW PICTURE OF HIMSELF.
HIS WANDERLUST STUCK, SO HE'S HARDLY HOME.
BUT I CAN'T GO AROUND LIKE THAT ANYMORE.
IT WAS FUN TO FLIT ABOUT FREELY LIKE A BIRD...
...BUT I HAVE SOMETHING MORE IMPORTANT NOW.
SINCE I'VE PLANTED MYSELF HERE...
...TO PROTECT IT...
...I CAN'T LEAVE ANYMORE.

...OKAY.
THOSE KIDS ARE GONE.

...OWW.

HM?
CRUMBLE
CRUMBLE

......
HUH ...?

!?
WHOOM

OH!
KURO-CHA!

OH, THAT ONE WAS BIG.
Maybe spring's getting close.
RUMBLE RUMBLE RUMBLE

SHUDDER
.......!

NIJUKU!
WHAT HAP-PENED TO YOUR FACE!?
GRAB
...?
WAIT. HUH ...?
OHH? SO, 'COS OF THAT SHOCK, YOU REGAINED YOUR MEMORIES? I'M GLAD FOR YOU.
It's like how you cure hiccups.
BUT WHY DO YOU LOOK SO UNCOM-FORTABLE? AREN'T YOU HAPPY?
HUH? OH... I AM.

WIPE
...WHEN YOU TRAVEL, YOU HAVE TO TRAVEL LIGHT.
THE MORE YOU HAVE, THE MORE DISTRACTING IT IS TO PROTECT. IT MAKES YOU LESS MOBILE.

...OH.
IT'S JUST SOOT...
WHAT'S SOOT?

BUT WITHOUT KNOWING IT...
...IT SEEMS MY LUGGAGE HAS GOTTEN TOO HEAVY.

YOU KNOW WHEN NIJUKU TURNED BLACK BECAUSE OF ME?
YEAH.
I remember that.
THE "ATTACK" MADE ME REALIZE THAT...
...AND I WAS WORRIED ABOUT CONTINUING THIS JOURNEY.
IT WAS REALLY SIMILAR ...
...TO WHEN I STOPPED BEING MYSELF BEFORE.
AS I SLEPT...
...I'M SURE I WAS WAVERING BETWEEN WHICH LUGGAGE TO KEEP AND WHICH TO LEAVE BEHIND.
FWIP
THAT'S WHY I THINK I WAS SCARED IN THE BACK OF MY MIND.
THAT I'D SOMEDAY DO TO THEM WHAT THE WITCH DID TO ME.
MY COFFIN OR THEM.
THERE'S GOING TO COME A TIME WHEN I HAVE TO CHOOSE ONE.

AND IF THAT HAPPENS ...
...I KNOW *I* WOULDN'T BE ABLE TO TURN BACK.
...BUT WHEN THAT TIME COMES...
...I REALLY DON'T KNOW WHAT I'M GOING TO DO.

...I DON'T GET IT.
YOU CAN'T HAVE BOTH?
It's a little late, but she realized that having both is a "conflict."
The weight of your luggage hasn't changed.
You just feel it's heavier now, that's all.
If she doesn't plan to die, she doesn't need to carry a coffin.
And if the kids are with her, she can't die.
It's true that they're our luggage.
But they think and act on their own.
Maybe the day'll come when they grow apart from us.
It's an awkward paradox.
Even that time a year ago, you were telling them to stay away.
This is your journey...
...as well as theirs.
They wanted to travel with you. That's why they waited for you to wake up.
But right before you fainted...
...what were you doing?
Kuro.
What do you want to do?

LOOK, THEY'RE AWAKE.
We could've waited until spring?
WHEN SEASONS CHANGE, OUR FEELINGS CHANGE.
I WANTED TO LEAVE BEFORE I CHANGED MY MIND.
GOOD MORNING, KURO-CHA!
WE'RE LEAVING ON OUR TRIP AGAIN, RIGHT?
EVER SINCE THAT DAY...
...WHEN I TOOK THEM OUTSIDE...
...MY ACTIONS WERE DECIDED.
....
NO MATTER WHAT HAPPENS TO ME...
...I NEED TO LAY DOWN A PATH FOR THEM...
YEAH.
...SO THAT THEY CAN CONTINUE ON THEIR OWN.

But don't push your-self too much.
Growing herbs was such a hassle. I don't wanna do it again.
Okay, okay.
Whistle
Whistle
Whistle
...That man...
Do you know him?
No.
Hunh?
I just saw him being stabbed many times.
With a knife.
Kuro-cha, hurry!
We found a store!
Hey, don't run ahead.
By the way, I heard a rumor.
There's a vampire that lurks around here...
Really? I wonder if it's true.
Ida! A cus-tomer!
Oh! Okayyy!
Hello!

THE "TORO-KUSHI GATHER-ING"?
THAT'S WHAT THIS PLACE IS CALLED?
Yeah.
We've luckily encountered them many times over the course of our travels.
They come in different shapes and sizes.
It could just be one rotting shack in a town...
...or it could be a community, like here.
It's like a "hideaway" that only a few travelers know about.
Those there welcome wanderers and travelers for some reason.
Some only stay temporarily to take shelter from the cold of winter or a storm...
...and some stay and bury their bones.
......
Why do you look like you're not convinced?
SO THE ENTIRE WORLD HAS A FREE INN FOR TRAVELERS SOMEWHERE?
ISN'T THAT UNFAIR?
A PRIVILEGE FOR MAIN CHARAC-TERS?
It's not like it's a villa for travelers.
That's only the end result.
KLUNK
In the beginning, it was just a resting place...
...for people with status and nobility.

And so the four shadows started walking again.
There are some things that haven't changed,
while it seems that other things have
changed dramatically.

A TOWN OR A VILLAGE AROUND HERE?
YEAH RIGHT, IN THE FOREST?

IF YOU DON'T MIND HOW CRAMPED IT IS, WE CAN TAKE YOU.
ON THAT.
HUH?

THE CLOSEST WOULD BE A THREE- NO, FOUR-DAY WALK FROM HERE.
THAT MANY ...?
WE THOUGHT WE COULD FIGURE IT OUT IF WE STAYED ALONG THE RIVER...

....
...A RAFT ...?

WOW! WOW!
WE'RE RUNNING ON THE WATER!
SPLASH
SPLASH
SPLASH
SPLASH

WE CAN SEE KURO-CHAN OVER THERE!
KURO-CHA! HEYYY!

Ha-Ha, look at them waving frantically.
Kuro, you should wave back...

WAVE...? A WHITE FLAG...?
OH, I forgot you get seasick.

I don't have mint, so chew on these leaves.
Only a little at a time now.
OH, OKAY.

IT'S NOT HELPING THAT I'M HUNGRY TOO...
We were running out of food and money. It was doubtful that we'd make it across the mountain.

IF THE MAN DIDN'T OFFER TO GIVE US A RIDE...
We would've just ended up bandits, that's all.

YEAH, GUESS SO.
HEY!
That was just a joke! You're s'posed to laugh!
C'MON!
MUST BE TOO SICK TO RESPOND PROPERLY.
CHEW CHEW
もぐもぐ

What are you doing?
You're not trying to catch fish with your bare hands, are you?

We're gonna arrive in town tomorrow morning.
Think you can hold on till then?
YEAH... I THINK I FEEL A LITTLE BETTER.

NO. THE MOON FLOATING IN THE RIVER WAS SHINY AND PRETTY.
SO I TRIED TO SCOOP IT UP.

I'M GLAD THEY TOOK THE KIDS ON THE BOAT.
YOU'LL FEEL BETTER IF YOU LOOK UP.
In this condition, you wouldn't be able to keep an eye on them.

BUT THEN, LOOK.
WHEN I TOUCH IT, IT BREAKS DOWN.

THEY DID JUMP INTO A LAKE IN AN ATTEMPT TO CATCH THE SKY REFLECTED IN IT AND ALL.
IF THEY WERE HERE, I WOULDN'T BE ABLE TO REST UNTIL MORNING.
Ha Ha Ha!

The moon in the water, flowers reflected in a mirror—
You think they're there and try to touch them...
...but they disappear immediately, and you realize it was an illusion.

But you did something like that a long time ago yourself.
HUH?
ME?

...WHO'S THERE?
WHOOSH

....
THE MOON REFLECTED ON THE WATER... EH?

GRAB
!!

...HM?

......
WHAT'S WITH YOU ...?

SPLOSH
チャプン

YOU'RE NOT FIGHTING BACK?
I'M BUSY FIGHTING A HEADACHE AND NAUSEA.
IF YOU CAN'T TELL.
DANGLE

SORRY, BUT I'M GONNA STAY ON THIS RAFT FOR A WHILE.
YOU GOT ANY SMOKES?
NO.

.........! GOLD ...!?
THAT'S RIGHT.
I DIDN'T THINK IT WAS REALLY HERE.

I DIDN'T THINK THERE WERE THIEVES IN THE RIVER.
WHICH DID YOU COME FOR? THE STEAMBOAT OR THE SEASICK TRAVELER?

I KNEW THERE WAS GOLD UP-STREAM.
NOT JUST ME. PEOPLE IN THE TOWN DOWNSTREAM HEARD ABOUT IT AND ARE SECRETLY AFTER IT.

YOU REALLY DON'T KNOW ANYTHING, EH?
SLASH

THIS BOAT'S OFFICIALLY CARRYING LUMBER...
...BUT SECRETLY CARRYING GOLD DUST.
....

LOOK.
THIS IS WHAT I CAME FOR.

I THOUGHT YOU WERE GUARDING THE GOLD.
AND THAT'S WHY YOU ATTACKED ME AS SOON AS YOU SAW ME, EH?

IS THAT WHY THEY KEPT NIJUKU AND SANJU ON THE BOAT?
EVEN IF WE'D SEEN THE GOLD DUST, WE COULDN'T HAVE MADE OFF WITH IT...
DAMMIT. EVEN IF I TAKE ALL THIS, IT WON'T AMOUNT TO MUCH.
DON'T THEY HAVE MORE HIDDEN SOMEWHERE ...?

I KNOW. LET'S MAKE A DEAL.
......A DEAL?
I WANNA MAKE MORE MONEY, AND I DON'T WANT YOU BLABBING ABOUT ME.
SUSPICION MIGHT FALL ON YOU, BUT CAN YOU LET ME GO AND KEEP MUM ABOUT ME?

WHOA! THE HELL? THIS IS A COFFIN!
THAT'S MINE.

IN RETURN, I'LL GIVE YOU HALF OF THE GOLD.
NOT A BAD DEAL FOR YOU, RIGHT?
YEAH, WE'LL MEET UP AT THE BRIDGE IN TOWN.

HUH. YOU SURE DO COME PREPARED, DON'T YOU?
......WHAT DO YOU MEAN?

YOU NEED TO LIVE ON SOME-THING TOO.
A HANDFUL OF THIS WILL WIPE HALF OF YOUR WORRIES AWAY.

NOT INTER-ESTED. DO WHAT YOU WANT.
I'M GOING TO SLEEP.
YAWN
WHAT!?
ARE YOU SERI-OUS?

HEH! SISSY.
DON'T REGRET IT WHEN YOU DIE PENNILESS ON THE ROAD.

I'M NOT GOING TO REACH FOR THE MOON IN THE WATER ANYMORE.
WHAT ARE YOU TALKING ABOUT?

HEY, WHAT IF INSTEAD...
...I OFFERED YOU THIS GOLD IN EXCHANGE FOR YOUR LUGGAGE?

IF I REACH FOR IT, THE MOON WILL DISAPPEAR.
AND ALL THAT WILL REMAIN IS MY SKEWED FACE IN THE WATER.

HUH?
NAH.
NEVER MIND.

I'LL THINK ABOUT WHAT I'D DO IF I HAD THE MOON BEFORE REACHING FOR IT.
UNTIL THEN, IT'S EASIER TO JUST GAZE ON IT FROM AFAR.

I'M GOING.
TO THE OTHER SIDE OF THE WATER'S SURFACE.

Kuro.
Kuro, wake up.
We can see the town.

CRAP!
DAZED
Uh...
You chewed up all the leaves!?

Hey, this is originally a painkiller.
If you take too much, it paralyzes your sensory nerves, and...

THE BAGS...
THEY'RE NOT RIPPED OPEN...

THANK YOU SO MUCH.
SO MUCH!
MUCH!
SURE. KIDS, MAKE SURE YOU LISTEN TO THIS FELLA!!

BY THE WAY, DON'T GO TO THE OTHER SIDE OF THAT BRIDGE THERE.
ALTHOUGH YOU WON'T FIND ANY-THING IF YOU DO.
THE BRIDGE ...?

DECADES AGO, IT WAS A BUSTLING RESIDENTIAL AREA.
RIGHT NOW, IT'S JUST A GHOST TOWN.
What was there before?

NOTHING.
JUST A BUNCH OF DREAMERS.

HUH? GOLD?
HM?
IT'S BEEN A WHILE SINCE I HEARD ABOUT THAT.
WHEN MY GRANDPA WAS ALIVE, WE HEARD STORIES ABOUT THERE BEING GOLD UP-RIVER.
AND MANY PEOPLE FLOCKED HERE, HOPING TO PAN FOR GOLD.
WAS IT A SIDE EFFECT OF THE HERBS?
OR WAS HE ATTRACTED BY THE COFFIN?
BUT IN THE END, I DON'T THINK ANYONE FOUND ANY. IT WAS JUST A DREAM.
SO NO ONE KNOWS IF THERE REALLY WAS GOLD IN THE FIRST PLACE.
IF I'D...
...REACHED FOR THE GOLD—
WHAT'S GOLD?
Magic that gives the illusion of finding Happiness.
NO, I SHOULDN'T THINK ABOUT IT.
IT WAS ALL JUST AN ILLUSION.

THIS AREA IS ALL VAGUE ON THE MAP.
AND IT'S A FAIRLY NEW MAP I JUST BOUGHT TOO.
I'm starving.
I hope we can get outta here today.
とんとん
KNOCK
KNOCK
EXCUSE MEEE!
PLEASE GIVE US FOOOOD!
Hey, they're probably some rich, sheltered family living out in the middle of nowhere.
There's no way they'll open their doors to a bunch of travelers.

OH?

I thought it was a rock wall, but it's a gate.

So there's a mansion this deep in the woods?

めぎょ

CRACK

SEE.

.... IT'S MORE OPEN THAN I EXPECTED ON THE INSIDE.

That said, it looks like the people who once lived here are long dead and gone.

IT DOESN'T SEEM LIKE ANYONE'S AROUND.
Man, I'm so Hungry.
HM?

ARE YOU... TRAVEL-ERS?

SOMETHING SMELLS YUMMY.
REALLY?
MAKE SURE YOU STAY WITHIN HEARING RANGE.

DIDN'T YOU SEE THE SIGNS ON YOUR WAY HERE?
Did you see any?
NO.

IT LOOKED FINE FROM THE OUTSIDE, BUT THE INSIDE IS PRETTY RUINED.
IT MUST HAVE BEEN A SPLENDID CASTLE BEFORE IT FELL.

THIS PLACE FORBADE CONTACT WITH OUT-SIDERS FOR A VERY LONG TIME.
IS THAT WHY IT WASN'T ON THE MAP?

FLAP
If the owner isn't Here, then I'll claim it and become the new king.
KING OF A CASTLE THAT'S EXPERIENCING A SEVERE FOOD SHORTAGE, YOUR HIGHNESS?

WHEN THE KING WAS STILL IN THE CASTLE...
...HE MET HIS DOOM BECAUSE OF ONE TRAVELER'S WORDS.

WHEN THIS CASTLE HAD A KING...
...IT WAS VERY SPLENDID AND OPULENT.

THIS KING LOVED TO HEAR TALES OF FOREIGN LANDS.

AND HE OFTEN INVITED TRAVELERS TO THE CASTLE TO HEAR THEIR STORIES.

THE KING WAS POMPOUS AND HATED TO LOSE.
HE WAS VERY GOOD AT GETTING ANYTHING HE WANTED.

THE COLORFUL FLOWERS THAT GREW ON THE SOUTHERN ISLANDS WERE SO BEAUTIFUL I CANNOT DO THEM JUSTICE WITH WORDS.
THOSE BLOOMS, COMFORTING ALL WHO BEHOLD THEM, ARE THE EPITOME OF TRUE BEAUTY.

IF HE HEARD A RUMOR THAT A KING IN THE FAR EAST...
...HAD A GOLDEN BIRD...

THE KING WAS NEVER INTERESTED IN FLOWERS BEFORE THAT.
BUT WHEN HE HEARD ANOTHER TELL OF HOW BEAUTIFUL THEY WERE, HE WANTED SOME FOR HIMSELF.

...A STATUE OF A LARGE GOLDEN PHOENIX WOULD BE STANDING ON THE SECOND TALLEST TOWER OF THE CASTLE...
...IN A MATTER OF DAYS.

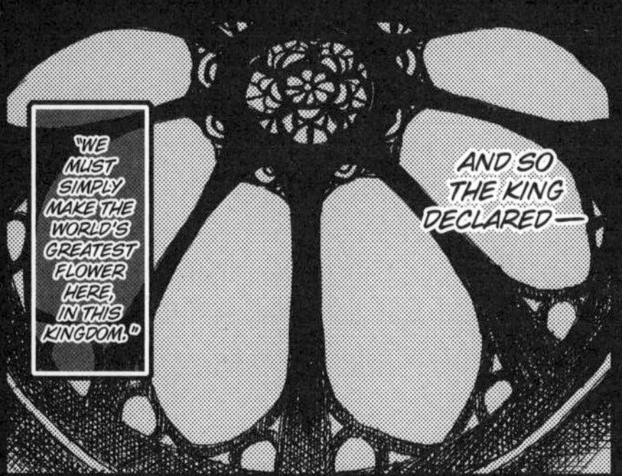
AND SO THE KING DECLARED—
"WE MUST SIMPLY MAKE THE WORLD'S GREATEST FLOWER HERE, IN THIS KINGDOM."

HE GATHERED ARTISTS, POETS, PHILOSOPHERS... ANYONE WHO DEEMED THEMSELVES EXPERTS IN BEAUTY.
AND HE ORDERED THEM TO CREATE A FLOWER THAT EXISTED NOWHERE ELSE.

AFTER MUCH RESEARCH AND MANY EXPERIMENTS...
...THEY CREATED JUST SUCH A FLOWER.

IT WAS BRIGHTER THAN THE SUMMER SUN.
DELICATE AS GLASSWORK.
SWEETER THAN A YOUNG COUPLE'S LOVE.

IT WAS A FLOWER UNLIKE ANY OTHER IN THE WORLD.
AND IT WOULD NEVER, EVER WILT.

THE KING WAS VERY SATISFIED WITH THIS FLOWER.
AT ONCE, HE DISPLAYED HIS PRECIOUS FLOWER FOR ALL TO SEE.

OF COURSE...
...THAT INCLUDED TRAVELERS AS WELL, SO THEY COULD SPREAD THE WORD ABOUT HIS FLOWER.
HOWEVER, THE TRAVELER SAID...

FORGIVE MY INSOLENCE, YOUR HIGHNESS.
HOWEVER, I DO NOT BELIEVE THAT THIS FLOWER IS THE GREATEST IN ALL THE WORLD.

I HAVE SEEN MANY MORE BEAUTIFUL ON MY JOURNEY.
AND THOSE FLOWERS CONTINUE TO BLOOM BOTH SOMEWHERE IN THE WORLD AND IN MY MEMORIES.

What an idiot, that traveler.
READ THE MOOD, WOULD YA?
I'm sure the king wasn't looking for an honest opinion.
How boorish of the king...
...to put a rank on the beauty of flowers.
YEAH, I GET THAT.
SO YOU AGREE WITH THE TRAVELER?
WELL, WE DON'T KNOW THE VALUE OF REFINED OBJECTS TO BEGIN WITH.
I HAVE A DETAILED MEMORY OF FLOWERS MYSELF...
WHILE PERHAPS NOT THE MOST BEAUTIFUL IN THE WORLD...
...IT WAS A TRULY BEAUTIFUL FLOWER FIELD.
You see it a lot with people who are always aiming for the best.
They plow their fields, swing their swords, and raise their children mindful of status and merit.
The beauty of a flower is in how fleeting it is and encountering it by chance.
Just like the landscape and the wind...
...'cos it's unique, it continues to blossom within your memories.
On the other hand, travelers hate following in line with the masses.
IT'S MORE CONVINCING COMING FROM A BAT.
That's why we're able to wander wherever, flitting this way and that.
CAN'T COMMIT TO ONE SIDE...
Just like a one-night stand with a woman tends to get beautifully etched into your memory too...
WON'T YOU CONTINUE WITH YOUR STORY?
AH.
I'm actually saying pretty deep and moving stuff here!

WHAT MADE THE KING GO TO SUCH LENGTHS TO ACHIEVE THESE ACCOLADES?
THE WORLD'S MOST BEAUTIFUL FLOWER...
THE WORLD'S MOST LUXURIOUS CASTLE. THE WORLD'S RAREST BIRD.
...AND THE WORLD'S GREATEST KING.
I HAVE TASKED YOU WITH CREATING THE BEST FLOWER IMAGINABLE. STOP EMBARRASSING ME!
IF YOU CAN'T DO IT, KEEP TRYING UNTIL YOU GET IT RIGHT!
THE KING KNEW.
ONLY AMIDST THESE VANITIES...
...WAS HIS POSITION ENABLED.
IF THEY RAN OUT OF FUNDS FOR THEIR RESEARCH, THEY CARVED AWAY THE GOLDEN WALLS OF THE CASTLE.
AND WHEN THEY NEEDED STILL MORE, THEY TOOK DOWN THE SCULPTURES AND TAPESTRIES.
BUT THE TRAVELER WAS DIFFERENT.
WALKING AS HE WISHED, SINGING AS HE PLEASED...
...HE SPOKE OF THE WORLD AS HE DESIRED.
AS LONG AS WE OBTAIN PRAISE, THAT BECOMES VALUE.
IMAGINARY MANIFESTATIONS BECOME BEAUTY.
A COMPLETE LIE CAN BECOME ART.
WHAT DID THE WIND THAT HAPPENED TO BRUSH AGAINST THE KING'S CHEEK...
...MAKE THE KING THINK OF?
WHAT IS THE MEANING OF...
...JEWELS YOU CAN'T WEAR OR PLAYS THAT DON'T MOVE YOU?
THEY'RE NAUGHT BUT RUBBISH!

And the result is this crumbling castle.

The only things driving the King were dignity and pride...
...as well as a little envy of those who were able to be free.

Do you think he finished the flower?
Well, his castle dropped off the face of the earth.
So there's your answer.

Your Highness, a traveler from a foreign land is here...
Silence! I don't want to be misguided by them right now!

Did you used to live in this castle?
My great-grandfather was the last resident here.
He was proud to be the gardener.

Don't allow any out-siders in.
I forbid them from entering this castle... No, this land!!

If you're still thinking of claiming this castle, I'll be your second in a duel.
Like I still want this place!
?
I'd forgotten all about that!

Until the world's best flower has been completed...
...I will deny entrance to even the wind!!

By the way, where are Nijuku and Sanju?
DARN, I TOTALLY FORGOT!
ACK.
THERE YOU ARE!
WHAT? YOU'RE STUCK AND CAN'T GET OUT?
I'll see if she can get out from the back.
NIJUKU! SANJU!
It's gonna be hard to find them in this vast place.
...I'M SURE THEY CAN'T HEAR ME.
WHAT WERE YOU DOING HERE?
I WAS FOLLOWING THE SMELL.
HAVE YOU SEEN TWO KIDS AROUND HERE?
EVEN IF YOU SAW ONE, THAT WOULD HELP.
A CHILD? NO, YOU'RE THE FIRST HUMAN I'VE SEEN IN A WHILE.
A SWEET SMELL.
?
LET'S SEE.
BUT NOT A FOOD SMELL.
OH, BUT...
...I DID SEE AN ANIMAL DUCK INTO SOME CREVICES IN THE RUBBLE.
It's gotta be them!
Hey, Kuro!
C'mere!

WOW...
IT'S LIKE A PALACE OF ROSES.
OH, RIGHT! YOU SAID YOU WERE A DESCENDANT OF THE CASTLE GARDENER.
DID YOU GROW THESE ...?

I'M ASHAMED YOU HAD TO SEE THIS.
ESPECIALLY SINCE YOU'RE THE FIRST GUESTS OF THIS CASTLE IN SEVERAL HUNDRED YEARS.
GROW THEM? OF COURSE NOT.
THESE ARE WEEDS.

I DON'T KNOW WHY YOU'RE SO EXCITED.
THESE HAVE ALWAYS BEEN HAZARDOUS WEEDS IN THIS COUNTRY.
THEIR SHARP THORNS DAMAGED THE CASTLE WALLS.
AND THEIR STRONG ODOR ATTRACTED INSECTS.
...AH, I SEE.
IT FINALLY MAKES SENSE.
What does?
PERHAPS BECAUSE OF THE RESEARCH AND EXPERIMENTS...
...THESE WEEDS ARE ESPECIALLY PERSISTENT AND POSSESS GREAT REPRODUCTIVE POWER.
THE MEMORY OF THE FLOWER FIELD...
...THAT STAYED IN MY MIND.
You mean... What you were talking about before?
AS MY GREAT-GRANDFATHER DID UNTIL HIS DYING DAY...
...I'VE KEPT CUTTING AWAY AT THEM.
BUT IT LOOKS LIKE THIS CASTLE WILL BE OVERTAKEN WITH THESE FLOWERS IN THE END.
IT WAS AN UNFORGETTABLE, BEAUTIFUL FIELD OF FLOWERS.
BUT NOW THAT I THINK ABOUT IT, THOSE WERE WILD GRASSES YOU MIGHT FIND ANYWHERE.
AND THEN, MAYBE THESE FLOWERS WILL HAVE THEIR REVENGE...
...AGAINST THE KING WHO TRIED TO CONTROL FLOWERS.
IT WASN'T...
...THE FLOWERS.
THAT MOMENT ITSELF WAS THE MOST BEAUTIFUL MEMORY I HAVE.

KURO-CHAN!
CAN YOU MAKE A CROWN WITH THESE FLOWERS?
THEY HAVE THORNS.
ME TOO! I WANT ONE TOO!
HM? NIJUKU.
YOU HAVE SOMETHING GLITTERY ON YOUR CLOTHES.
YeaH. YOU Have golden DUST on YOU.
ARE THEY PETALS? THEY LOOK LIKE GLASS.
MAYBE IT'S THAT.
WHAT WE FOUND IN THE PLACE YOU GOT STUCK.
RIGHT?
IT WAS SHINY AND PRETTY.
RIGHT.
...THat's PROLLY...
...naH, never mind.
BUT IT BROKE INTO PIECES.
PAT
PAT
WHen no one's around anymore...
...WHat do you tHink Will Happen to tHat castle?
I DON'T KNOW.
BUT...
...I THINK I'D LIKE TO SEE...
...THE RUINS OF AN OLD CASTLE BURIED IN WILD ROSES.
AND DECADES, CENTURIES LATER...
...MAYBE IT'LL BECOME PART OF A TRAVELER'S SONG.
ALTHOUGH it's a little different from WHat that king wanted.
THAT'S OKAY.
IT HAS VALUE BECAUSE ONE WILL SEE IT BY CHANCE.

SORRY ABOUT THE MESS.
BUT I THINK I HAVE EVERYTHING AVAILABLE.
I WISH YOU WOULD'VE categorized them by era.
It's Hard to tell what's old and what's new.
I CAN'T LET YOU TAKE ANY, BUT IF YOU NEED ONE, I CAN COPY IT FOR YOU.
WHAT MAP IS THAT?
AH, THIS IS THE "FIRST CONTI-NENT."
HOW NOSTALGIC. I COPIED IT WHEN I WAS A KID.
THE FIRST CONTI-NENT?
THE WORLD BEGAN AS ONE CONTINENT.
AND THERE WAS A LARGE KINGDOM.
BUT IT BECAME TOO BIG...
...AND ONE DAY, THE KINGDOM, CASTLE, PEOPLE, ANIMALS, MOUNTAINS, FORESTS, RIVERS...
...ALL FELL APART AND CRUMBLED.
AND THEN IN THE END, THEY DISAPPEARED AND WERE FORGOT-TEN.
It's not a PHantom land or something from the occult?
THE FIRST CONTINENT. I WOULD'VE LIKED TO SEE IT.
ME TOO.
BUT IF IT REALLY EXISTED...
...MAYBE A DESCENDANT OF THE OLD KINGDOM...
...IS STILL WALKING AROUND THE WORLD TODAY.

Shoulder-a-Coffin Kuro by Satoko Kiyuduki

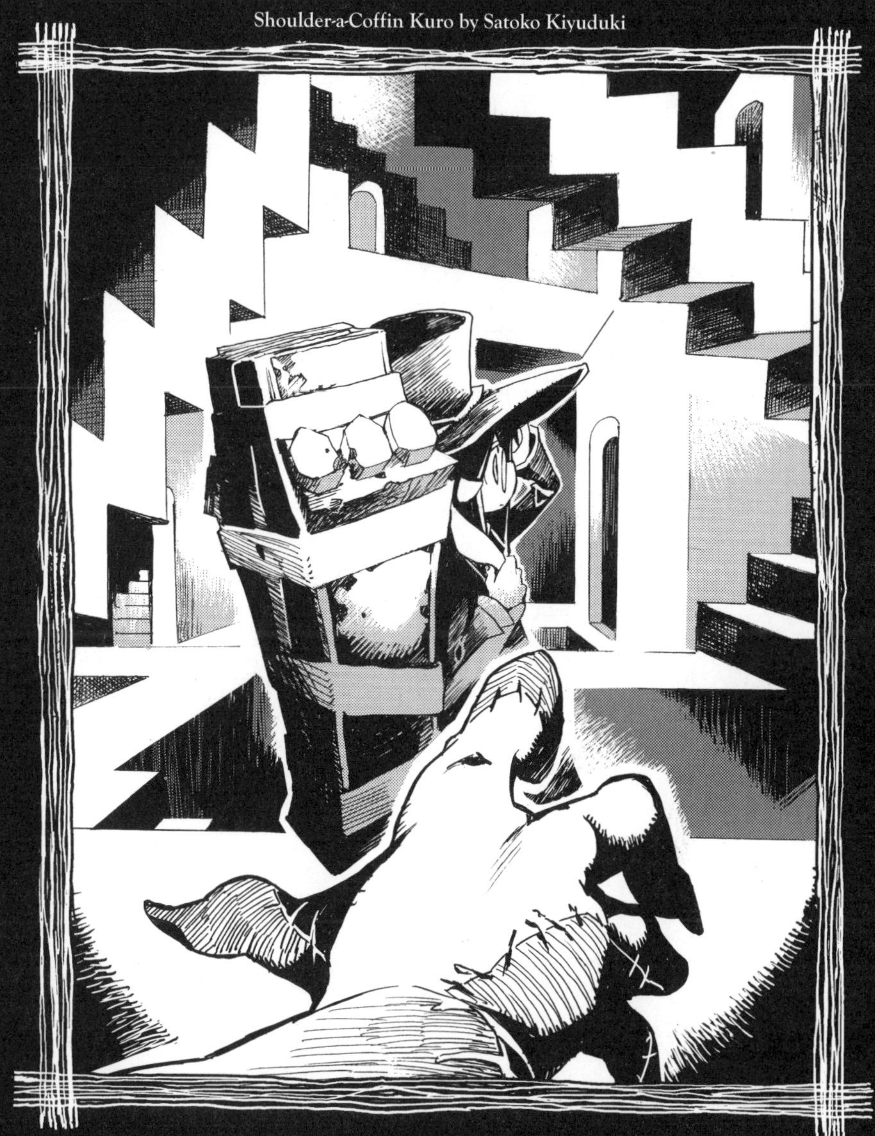

I looked up at the ceiling only to discover it was the floor.
I thought I ran up the stairs, but I had descended instead.
The door I opened thinking it was the exit was an entrance.

I thought I was the pursuer,
but it could be that I was being pursued.

WE'RE GOING, MARIA.
I'LL FINISH THIS BENCH WHEN WE COME BACK.

WE HAVE TO GO WORK IN A COUNTRY FAR AWAY...
...BUT WE'LL COME HOME AFTER A YEAR.

I WANT TO GO TOO.
NO, WE CAN'T TAKE YOU.
MAKE SURE TO BE GOOD AND LISTEN TO YOUR GRAND-MOTHER.

IT'S A PROMISE. WAIT FOR US ON TOP OF THIS HILL.
I'LL COME AND GET YOU AS SOON AS WE RETURN.
OKAY.
HURRY BACK!

—AND HERE ON THIS SPOT, WHERE I PROMISED MY MOTHER AND FATHER...

...I WAITED FOR A LONG, LONG TIME.

MARIA, YOU'RE GOING AGAIN TODAY?
IT'S ONLY BEEN A WEEK. THEY WON'T BE BACK YET.
I'M GOING ANYWAY!
!
THERE'S SOME-ONE THERE!
YOUR DAD MADE THIS BENCH, RIGHT?
THE EDGES AREN'T FINISHED. DID HE USE THE WHOLE TREE?
OW! OUCH!!
WHAT'RE YOU DOING? STOP PULLING ME!!
TUG TUG TUG TUG
GET OFF THE BENCH!!
YOU IDIOT!!
I SEE. YOUR PARENTS WENT OUT TO WORK TOO?
YEAH.
BUT THEY SAID THEY'D BE BACK SOON.
ALL THE YOUNG PEOPLE'RE GOING TO THE CITY TO EARN MONEY.
THAT'S WHAT MY DAD SAID.
ARE YOUR MOMMY AND DADDY GOING TOO?
NO, WE HAVE THE RANCH.
AND THEY'RE NOT SCHOLARS OR ANY-THING.
SO DON'T WORRY!
I'LL STAY WITH YOU FOREVER!
SMILE
I DON'T NEED YOU!
THEY'LL BE BACK ANY DAY NOW!

A YEAR PASSED QUICKLY.
BUT EVEN IN THE SECOND YEAR, THERE WAS NO SIGN OF THEIR RETURN.

!!

"WE HAD TO GO BEYOND THE SEA...
"...TO FIND WORK."
WHAT'S A "POPE" ...?

OH!
THE GODDESS ON THIS CARD...
...IF YOU CHANGE HER HAIR COLOR, SHE'LL LOOK LIKE MAMA!

HELLO.
IT'S NICE AND SHADY HERE.

NO, MAYBE HER EYES?
MAYBE HER NOSE IS DIFFERENT TOO.
WHAT DID MAMA LOOK LIKE?

....
?

I SEE. YOU'RE WAITING FOR YOUR PARENTS WHO WENT ABROAD TO COME BACK.
DID YOU COME FROM FAR AWAY TOO?
DID YOU SEE MY PARENTS?
UM... THEY'RE HERE!
FLAP
HM, I DON'T KNOW.
I CAME FROM THE OPPOSITE DIRECTION.
BUT I HAVE A DAUGHTER YOUR AGE.
I'M ABOUT TO GO SEE HER.
REALLY!?
I'M GOING TO GO PICK UP MY CHILD.
SO YOU SHOULD BE A GOOD GIRL AND WAIT FOR YOUR PARENTS TOO.
OKAY!!
THEN IT'S A RACE TO SEE WHICH OF US WILL SEE THEM FIRST!
HEY, MARIA?
ARE YOU GOING TO THE HILL TODAY TOO?
DASH
DEAR GOD, IF YOU CAN HEAR MY WISH...
SNIFF
...I CAN LIVE WITH MOTHER AND FATHER COMING HOME LATER.
SO PLEASE MAKE SURE...
...MY PARENTS DON'T GO SEE GRANDMA FIRST.

!
SNORE
SNORE
SOME-ONE'S THERE, BUT...
...IT'S PROBABLY SOMEONE ELSE AGAIN.
HIS LEGS ARE STICKING OUT...
SMOKE
SMOKE
....
HUH? WHAT THE—?
I SEE. YOU'RE WAITING FOR SOMEONE, AND YOU DON'T KNOW WHEN THEY'RE COMING BACK.
I THINK YOU'RE WASTING YOUR TIME.
WHAT ...!?
HOW COULD YOU SAY IT'S A WASTE!?
THE HOLY MOTHER GAVE LIFE TO THE DAUGHTER.
BUT SHE FORGOT TO GIVE HER HAPPINESS.
DO YOU KNOW THIS SONG?
NO. IS IT POPULAR?
EVEN WHEN YOU GO FISHING, YOU HAVE TO GO TO THE LAKE, OR THE FISH WON'T COME.
DON'T YOU THINK IT'S ABOUT TIME YOU WENT LOOKING FOR THEM?
I CAN'T DO THAT!
WE PROMISED THAT I WOULD "WAIT" HERE.
A TRAVELER LIKE YOU CAN MOVE ABOUT FREELY LIKE A BALLOON.
THAT'S WHY IT'S SO EASY FOR YOU TO SAY.
THAT LINE OF THOUGHT ...
...IS JUST YOU TAKING THE EASY WAY OUT.

AND THEN TIME FLEW BY AGAIN...
...AND TWELVE YEARS PASSED.

MARIA, I NEED TO TALK TO YOU.
WHAT? ANOTHER LECTURE FOR ME?
I'VE ALREADY FINISHED MY SEAM-STRESS WORK FOR TODAY, YOU KNOW.

THE RANCH IS VERY QUIET TODAY.
IS EVERY-ONE IN THE BARN?
...NO.

WE SOLD THE CATTLE.
OUR FAMILY MADE A DECISION TOO.
MARIA, WHAT WILL YOU DO?

HELLO.

WHO ARE YOU ...?
I GOT SEPARATED FROM MY COMPANION.
I HAVE A GOOD VIEW HERE, SO I THOUGHT IT WOULD BE EASY FOR ME TO FIND HIM.

AH, IS THE COFFIN IN YOUR WAY?
LET ME MOVE IT.
NO, IT'S OKAY!
THIS BENCH SEATS THREE!!

MY FATHER BUILT THIS BENCH ...
...SO THAT THE THREE MEMBERS OF OUR FAMILY COULD SIT HERE.
I SEE ...

YOU'RE WAITING FOR YOUR COMPAN-ION?
HMM ......
AREN'T YOU WORRIED, WAITING ALONE?
NOT REALLY.

BUT WE NEVER GOT THE CHANCE...
...TO SIT HERE TOGETH-ER.

I DO THINK IT'S A HASSLE.
BECAUSE I CAN'T MOVE FROM HERE.
HEE HEE, I'M JEAL-OUS.
YOU BELIEVE IN YOUR FRIEND.

EVERYONE IS SLOWLY MOVING OUT OF THIS VILLAGE ...
...IN SEARCH OF A NEW LIFE IN A NEW LAND.

WHENEVER I SAT HERE, WAITING, I FELT CONNECTED TO THEM.
BECAUSE "WAITING" IS SOME-THING...
...YOU CAN'T DO ALONE.

THE PEOPLE WHO SIT HERE...
...ALSO GET UP AND LEAVE IN THE END...

BUT STILL...
...WHEN YOU GET ANXIOUS ABOUT WAITING ...
...THAT IS TRULY THE LONELIEST THING.

...ARE YOU WAITING FOR SOMEONE TOO?
...OH, YES.
I'M WAITING FOR MY PARENTS.

...HUH?
I'M A MORTI-CIAN.
I FORGOT WHERE, BUT I REMEMBER SEEING THESE NAMES.

THIS WAS THEIR LAST LETTER TO ME.
THEY PROMISED TO COME AND GET ME...

Hey!
Finally found ya.
OH.
HE REALIZED I WAS HERE AT LAST.

...OH.

WELL, BYE.
SORRY FOR YOUR LOSS, BUT DON'T BE DISCOUR-AGED.

THESE TWO...
...PASSED AWAY.

OH...
....

When you're waiting, it must be easy.
WHAT A PAIN.
The one looking has to do all the work.
OH?
THERE'S A LOT OF DRAMA FOR THE WAITING PARTY TOO.

"THAT'S A LIE."
"I KNOW THEY'RE COMING BACK."
WHY COULDN'T I DENY WHAT SHE SAID?

NOT KNOWING IF THE OTHER IS DEAD OR ALIVE ...
...OR IF THEY'VE ABAN-DONED OR BETRAYED YOU.
YOU CAN ONLY WAIT WHILE BATTLING DOUBTS.
I WASN'T GONE THAT LONG!
HUH? What the heck?
You were that worried?

I KNEW...
...THAT WHAT SHE SAID WAS FALSE.

THE HOLY MOTHER GAVE LIFE TO THE DAUGHTER
BUT SHE FORGOT TO GIVE HER HAPPINESS.
OH?

SHE TESTED ME...
...TO SEE WHAT I WOULD SAY WHEN PROVOKED.

I think I've heard that before.
Where was it?
I DON'T REMEM-BER EITHER.
IT JUST POPPED INTO MY HEAD SUD-DENLY.

AND I COULDN'T REPLY.
THAT WAS MY "ANSWER."

YOU SURE YOU'RE OKAY WITH THIS?
YES.
I'VE MADE MY DECISION.

NO MATTER WHAT I CHOOSE...
...I'LL PROBABLY REGRET IT ONE WAY OR ANOTHER.

THAT'S WHY...

—Y!
HEY, MARIA!

WE'RE LEAVING!
COMING!!

THE PERSON IN ROOM 217 LEFT IN THE MIDDLE OF THE NIGHT.
AND THAT WAS ABOUT THREE YEARS AGO.
OH NO, THIS ADDRESS TOO?
THEY SAID IT WAS AN EMERGENCY.
WHAT ARE THE CHANCES OF SEEING A PERSON...
What's wrong?
...WHEN YOU DON'T KNOW WHERE HE OR SHE IS?
Well, you won't see them unless you're willing to.
And even if you don't will it, you might bump into them.
So even if the possibility of that happening is 29 out of 100...
GLANCE
WHY ARE YOU LOOKING AT ME?
...if that's the chance of seeing "her"...
...What will you do?
......I HAVE TO KEEP GOING TO GET CLOSE TO 100.
So there you go.
RIGHT?
Well, just aim for a ninety-six percent chance.
WHERE DID YOU GET THAT NUMBER?

THERE WAS A SICK MAN WHO WANDERED AROUND AIMLESSLY LATE AT NIGHT IN THE ALLEYS.

HE WAS SEARCHING FOR HIS SON, WHO WENT OUT TO BUY MEDICINE FOR HIS FATHER'S ILLNESS THREE DAYS EARLIER.

WHEN THE MAN SAW A STATUE OF A GODDESS ON THE STREET, HE FELL TO HIS KNEES AND PRAYED.

"DO YOU KNOW WHERE MY SON HAS GONE? PLEASE TELL ME."

THEN, A MYSTERIOUS THING TOOK PLACE.

THE STATUE ROSE AND TOOK FLIGHT.

THE GODDESS CAME BACK WITH HIS SON, WHO HAD FALLEN ASLEEP FROM FATIGUE.

AND FROM THAT MOMENT ON, THE MAN WAS CURED OF HIS ILLNESS.

THAT'S HOW THIS TOWN GOT THE REPUTATION OF HAVING MIRACLES.

SO IT SAYS.

WOW, THEY EVEN HAVE A GUIDEBOOK?

THERE'RE A LOT OF TOURISTS.
DO YOU THINK THAT ANECDOTE IS ENOUGH TO ATTRACT THIS MANY PEOPLE?

SO DID YOU COME HERE TO RELY ON THE POWER OF MIRACLES TOO?
NO AT ALL.
BESIDES, I DIDN'T KNOW ABOUT IT UNTIL I READ THIS.

BUT IT'S TRUE...
...THAT I WAS GUIDED TO THIS TOWN BY ITS POWER.
GUIDED?

THERE WAS A BUS...
...FROM THE PREVIOUS TOWN HERE.
THEY LET ME ON FOR FREE.
I SEE...
POWER AS IN MONEY POWER.

TOWN OF MIRACLES.
WHAT'S A MIRACLE?
LET'S ASK KURO-CHA AND SEN.

KURO-CHAN, WHAT'S A MIRACLE?
HM? UH...
SOMETHING THAT CAN'T HAPPEN IN NORMAL CIRCUMSTANCES.

WHAT'S SOMETHING THAT CAN'T HAPPEN IN NORMAL CIRCUMSTANCES?
HUH? WELL ...
YOU TWO, FOR EXAMPLE.

WE'RE THE MIRACLES.
SO THIS IS OUR TOWN?

NIJUKU, SANJU, WE'RE GOING.
'KAYY!

There sure are a lot of forks in the road.
HEY, DON'T RUN AHEAD.

BEFORE US IS THE OLD CASTLE TOWN.
I see. Maybe there's touristy stuff there.

OH?
Where'd the little ones go?
THEY RAN AHEAD.

HUH? THEY'RE NOT COMING?
THESE PEOPLE DON'T MOVE.

SEN, WAIT.
WE ALREADY WENT THAT WAY.
seriously?

THERE THEY ARE!
OVER HERE!

THIS IS FUN.
YEAH!
NOW I get...
...HOW the son got lost.

SEE, THERE'S AN OLD CASTLE OVER THERE.
YEAH, I SEE IT.
WELL, JUST LIKE THE MAN SAID...
THERE ARE A LOT OF NICE-LOOKING STATUES ALL OVER THE PLACE.
THIS TOWN WAS A COMMUNITY MADE UP OF RESIDENCES AND WORK-SHOPS...
...FOR THE WORKERS AND ARTISANS HIRED TO BUILD THE CASTLE.
I SEE. THAT'S HOW IT STARTED.
KURO-CHA, WE FOUND ANOTHER ONE.
OKAY.
...WHAT ARE YOU ALL DOING?
SO IS THE CASTLE BUILT ALL CONVOLUTED TOO?
OF COURSE NOT. THE CASTLE CONSTRUCTION IS SIMPLE.
AS FAR AS THE CASTLE TOWN GOES...
STAMP
21
58
...IT'S THE RESULT OF ITS RESIDENTS TRYING TO MAKE THEIR AREA LOOK BETTER.
THE RESIDENTS ARE ALL VAIN.
I GUESS THAT'S WHAT HAPPENS WHEN YOU HAVE A TOWN FULL OF ARTISANS.
WE GET A FREE STAY IF WE COLLECT ALL THE STAMPS.
HUH...
I'M GONNA STAMP THE NEXT ONE!

But it's weird. We've been all over...
...but we haven't seen the statue of the goddess.
YEAH.
WHAT KINDA GODDESS ?
DOES IT LOOK LIKE THIS?
THAT'S RIGHT. THIS TOWN *DOESN'T HAVE A STATUE OF THE GOD-DESS.*
HUH? What the heck?
OR MORE ACCURATELY, NO ONE'S FOUND IT YET.
SEN! SEN!
WHICH DO YOU THINK IS THE REAL GODDESS?
WHAT'RE YOU DOING, BRINGING OUT YOUR WINGS...?
Didja think I was gonna say the middle one?
BUT THIS TOWN HAS SO MANY BUILDINGS AND STATUES.
IT WOULDN'T BE SURPRISING IF THE GODDESS IS HIDDEN IN A CORNER SOMEWHERE.
SO THE MYSTERY OF THE GODDESS AND THE MIRACLE TALE...
...ARE WHAT DROVE PEOPLE TO FLOCK HERE.
IT'S GETTING DARK.
Play-time's over. Let's go!
AND THE TOWN IS OFFERING A REWARD TO ANYONE WHO FINDS IT.
I thought this place was better than that.
YOU GET FIFTY GOLD COINS.
HM?
There's an extra one.

DO YOU THINK SHE'S LOST?
Well, I'm not surprised. It's this town we're talking about.
DO YOU KNOW WHERE YOUR FAMILY WAS HEADED?
ARE YOU MEETING THEM SOME-WHERE?
I CAME WITH MY MUMMY TO SEE THE GODDESS.
MY BIG BROTHER IS SICK, AND WE NEED MONEY TO MAKE HIM BETTER.
BUT WE DON'T HAVE ANY.
So you held on to the vague hope of the miracle, eh?
BUT I FOUND THE GODDESS, SO IT'S OKAY!
THE GODDESS COULD BRING MY MUMMY HERE TOO.
MUMMY?
NOW WHAT ...?
Isn't there an info center here or some-thing?
This is a tourist trap, after all.
THEY'RE CLOSED BY NOW, SURELY.
OH, BUT...
...THERE WAS A VIGILANTE CORPS OFFICE AT THE TOWN ENTRANCE.
Okay, let's go there.
YOU THREE STAY HERE AND STAY PUT.
OKAY!
You're not gonna take them?
I DON'T KNOW IF I CAN GET THERE *SAFELY.*
We have to go through that maze again, eh?
URGH...
WE MIGHT GET LOST TOO.

WOW, GODDESS!
YOU GOT THIS MANY STAMPS?
YEAH.
BUT WE DON'T HAVE THE LAST ONE.

HEY! THERE'S SOME-THING GOING ON!
BUZZ
COME OUT AND LOOK!!
BUZZ

OH! NIJUKU!
THERE'S A STONE PERSON OVER THERE!
YOU'RE RIGHT. MAYBE THERE'S A STAMP!

I'M NOT SEEING THINGS, RIGHT?
BUZZ
BUZZ
SEN...
Yeah, we need to get back.

IT'S DARK, AND WE CAN'T SEE.
LIGHT?
WE NEED LIGHT...

WILL THIS DO?
SHINE
OH! NOW WE CAN SEE!

NOW those idiots've Done it...

WORD OF THE GODDESS'S APPEARANCE SPREAD THROUGH THE TOWN OVERNIGHT.
AND THE TRAVELERS LEFT AS IF THEY WERE RUNNING AWAY FROM THE MIRACLE.

What're we gonna do?
Everyone's saying it's a miracle and making a fuss.
WHY?
THE MIRACLE IS US, RIGHT?

AS THE ONLY ONE TO MEET AND BE SAVED BY THE GODDESS, THE LITTLE GIRL'S STORY INSPIRED MANY.
AND SHE AND HER MOTHER WERE REWARDED HAND-SOMELY.
?

WELL, AT LEAST IT HELPED THE MOTHER FIND HER DAUGH-TER.
All's well that ends well, eh?

THE LOCAL ARTISANS, WHO WERE SKEPTICAL ABOUT THE MIRACLE...
...ALL BEGAN TO MAKE GODDESS STATUES.

I'm tired. I need to get some sleep.
LOOK, I GOT ALL THE STAMPS!

AND THE TOWN CAME TO BE KNOWN AS THE TOWN OF "ODD STATUES" WHERE GOD-DESSES COEXISTED WITH THE PEOPLE.
BUT THAT'S ANOTHER STORY.

BUT...
...I WONDER WHERE THAT REALLY SHINY LIGHT CAME FROM ...?

NI-
JUKU.
LET'S
PLAY.
WHAT
WE PLAYED
YESTER-
DAY!
YOU'RE
DONE FOR
TODAY.
PRO-
FESSOR
SAID.
GLUG
コポ
コポ
GLUG
TAP
コッ
YOU
LIKE
IT?
BOBBLE
BOBBLE?
LIKE
THE
FIRST
TIME?
...?
YOU
WANT
TO STAY
THERE?
NO?
WHY
NOT?
PRO-
FES-
SOR.
PRO-
FES-
SOR.
I WANT
TO BE
SOMETHING
DIFFERENT
TOO.
......
....
GLUG
コポ...
WHAT'S
WRONG,
NIJUKU?
ARE YOU
SLEEPY?

NO!
A LITTLE LONGER!
Hey.
Let's give up already.
IT'S FINE, SEN.
THERE'S STILL TIME.
It's not a big deal.
Even if you can't find it, it's not like you're gonna die.
NO!
JUST A LITTLE LONGER!
In the first place, it's all your fault...
...for finding this.

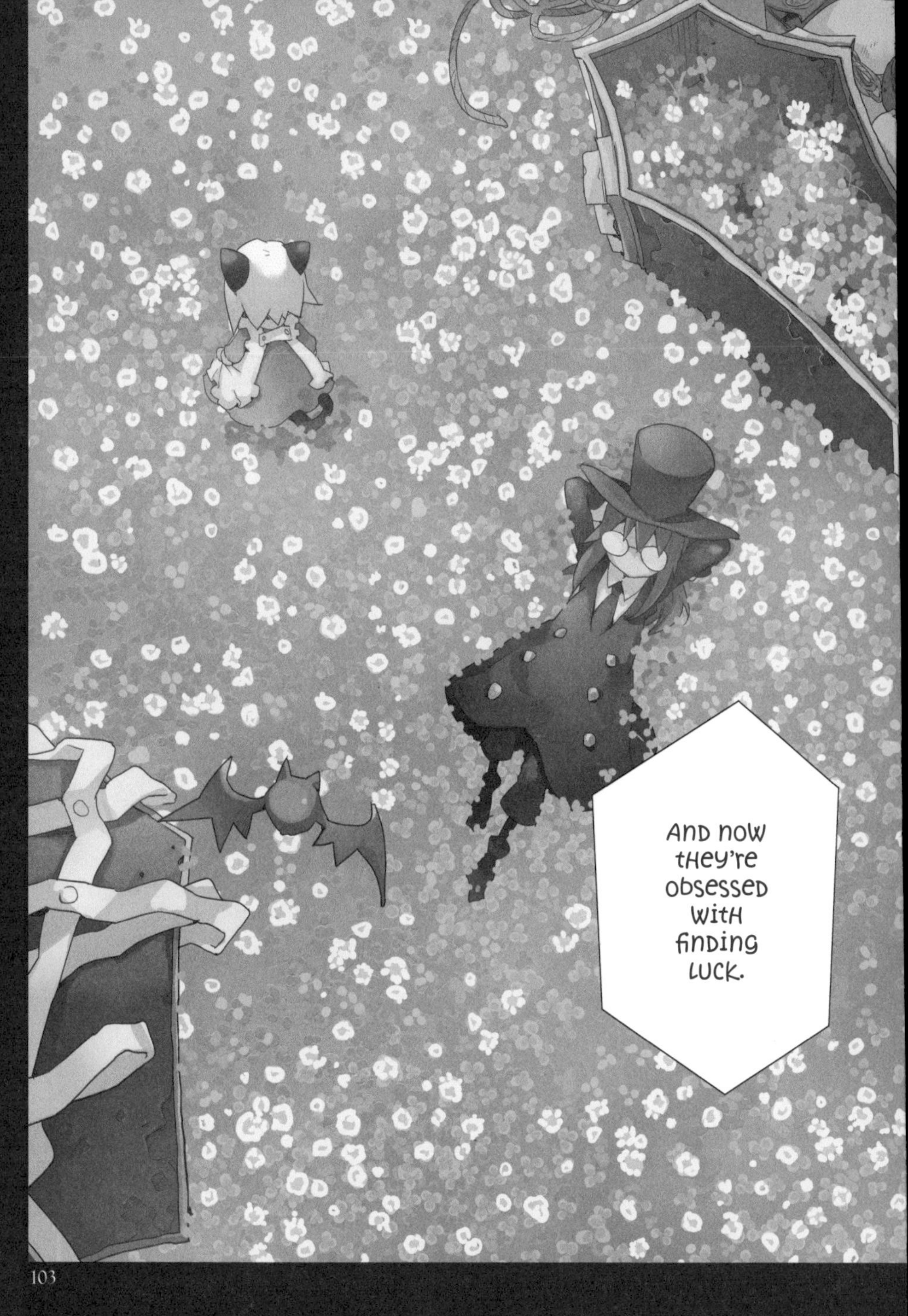
And now they're obsessed with finding luck.

A FEW HOURS AGO
SPLASH
THE BELT WAS LOOSE.
DID THE WHOLE THING GET WET?
CAN YOU TWO PICK SOME DRIED GRASS FOR ME?
WE'LL USE IT TO SOAK UP THE WATER IN THE COFFIN.
'KAYY!
So this place has been overrun with white clover.
WHITE?
OH, WAIT.
I FOUND A FOUR-LEAF CLOVER.
You found luck.
CLOVER?
?
SEE, THERE ARE FOUR LEAVES.
YEAH, IT'S DIFFER-ENT.
DIF-FERENT FROM WHAT WE HAVE.
YEAH. BECAUSE IT'S RARE AND UN-COMMON...
...THEY SAY YOU'LL GET GOOD LUCK IF YOU FIND IT.
GOOD LUCK?
LET'S FIND MORE!
THERE ARE NONE. NONE.
NO FOUR-LEAFS.
BUT IF WE DON'T FIND IT...
...GOOD LUCK WON'T COME.
I KNOW!
IF THE GOOD LUCK COMES FIRST...
...WE CAN FIND A FOUR-LEAF.
OH YEAH!
THEN LET'S GO LOOK FOR GOOD LUCK TO FIND THE FOUR-LEAF.
Don't you guys ever think about what you're saying?

KURO-CHAN, KURO-CHAN.
HM...?
PAT
PAT
CAN YOU MOVE?
OH.
SORRY.
I CAN'T FIND THE FOUR-LEAF.
NO! KURO-CHA.
DON'T COME THIS WAY!
WHOA!?
......
ALL THE SAME, IT'S...
...REALLY NICE OUT TODAY.
IS THAT WHY YOU'RE SO SLEEPY?
WHEN I SMELL THE GRASSY SCENT OF WHITE CLOVERS...
...FOR SOME REASON, I GET SLEEPY.
DID THIS PLANT HAVE THAT EFFECT?
OR IT IS A SECONDARY SYMPTOM OF HAY FEVER?
NO, IT'S NOT LIKE THAT.
I DON'T KNOW. IT'S NOSTAL-GIC.
MAKES ME RELAX.

HUH? HUH?
DID KURO-CHAN GO TO SLEEP?
OH.
You finally find a four-leaf clover?

NOT YET.
I HAVE A BUNCH OF MISSES.
BUNCH
It SHOWS tHat any good luck requires sacrifice.
GREED IS A SIN.

CAN I PUT IT HERE...
...TO SEPARATE THEM?
THat's fine, but...

...it's starting to look like a funeral.

......
HM...?

NIJUKU? SANJU?
WHAT IS IT THIS TIME?

OH!
I...
...FINALLY FOUND YOU! HIFUMI!

CREEP
DID YOU FOR-GET...
...WHAT I SAID THEN?
CREEP

BREAK THE CURSE YOU PUT ON ME.
IT'S THE ONLY REASON I'VE BEEN LOOKING FOR YOU ALL THIS TIME.

WAIT!
WHAT DO YOU...

LOOK-ING?
WHY WERE YOU LOOKING FOR ME?

...MEAN—?

I AM YOU.
WE'VE ALWAYS BEEN TOGETH-ER.
ALWAYS.

MMFGH!
RISE
OH? You're awake?

KOFF! KOFF!
Hey, Don't bury Her face too.
THEN SHE REALLY WILL DIE.
FOUND IT!
WHOOSH
FOUR-LEAF!
REALLY!?
LOOK, KURO-CHA!
......
IT SURE IS...
...BUT PEOPLE OFTEN GET THE TWO CONFUSED ...
CLOVER AND OXALIS.
OX?
HUH.
Even these Have meaning in the language of flowers?
YEAH.
LAN-GUAGE?
WHITE CLOVER SYMBOL-IZES...
..."PROM-ISE."
A FOUR-LEAF CLOVER MEANS ...
..."BE MINE."
OH? THat's a three-leaf.
Where'd the four-leaf go?
OH.
GUESS I LOST IT.

PROFES-SOR. PROFES-SOR.
WHAT? SANJU, IT ***FELL OFF*** AGAIN?
FALLING OFF IS BAD?
WHY?
HM?
ISN'T THAT OBVIOUS?

YOU REALLY ARE A HANDFUL.
I PUT IT TOGETHER OVER AND OVER, BUT THIS NEVER ENDS.
YOU NEED TO BE MORE CAREFUL.
PUTTING BACK WHAT YOU LOST...
...IS A HASSLE. THAT'S WHY.

Isn't...
...it obvious?
You said your feet hurt from walking too much yesterday.
You're gonna start whining that it hurts or you're tired again.
So if you can fix it with medicine, it's better to take it.
NO!
If you're good, you'll take your medicine.
C'mon.
YOU'RE LYING!
YOU HAVE THE LIE FACE!
YOU CAN TAKE IT FIRST!
NIJUKU, PULL HARDER!
OWWWWW, MY WINGS! MY WINGS!
TUGGG
YAWN
I SEE. THEY LEFT?
NO WONDER IT'S SO QUIET.
Sanju doesn't pull any punches when she wants her way.
I really thought my wings were gonna tear off.
I SEE...
OH WELL.
I didn't think it'd have a normal effect on them anyway.
WHERE DID YOU GET THESE PILLS?
ARE THESE THE INSTRUCTIONS?
"WANTED: TEST SUBJECTS FOR A BRAND-NEW PAIN-KILLER."
I SEE.
I thought it'd pay for some booze.
JANGLE

SEE?
IT LANDS WHEN YOU DO THIS.
I WANT IT TOO!
I WANT TO TOUCH IT TOO!
NO.
YOU SQUEEZE TOO HARD.
NIJUKU, YOU MEANIE!
YOU HAVE TO BE NICE IF YOU'RE OLDER!
SIS, I FOUND 'EM!
I FOUND SOME GIRLS!
HUH?
WHERE DID YOU COME FROM?
THIS DISTRICT ONLY HAS BOYS, AND WE DON'T HAVE ANYONE TO PLAY WITH.
SO LET'S PLAY!
WELCOME, MRS. GREEN DRESS!
WOULD YOU LIKE SOME TEA AND CAKE?
SIS!!
LOOK, SHE TORE ELIZA-BETH'S ARM.
IT FELL OFF.
OH NO!
IT CAN'T BE HELPED. THIS DOLL IS OLD.
DON'T WORRY. MOM CAN FIX IT.
MOM IS PROFES-SOR?
HUH? WHAT DO YOU MEAN?

AND THEN WE HAD TEA WITH THE DOLLS.
THEY ASKED US TO COME AGAIN!
I SEE. THAT'S GREAT.
YOU TWO MADE FRIENDS.
FRIENDS?
WHAT ARE FRIENDS?
PEOPLE WHO YOU PROMISE TO PLAY WITH AGAIN.
NOW GO TO SLEEP, SO YOU CAN PLAY AGAIN TOMORROW.
OKAY!
HUH?
SEN'RS SLEEPING ALREADY?
YEAH, HE HAS A TUMMY ACHE.
EMPTY
HOW CUTE!
I WANT TO HOLD IT NEXT!
WHAT ARE YOU DOING?
OH, HELLO AGAIN!
LOOK!
WE GOT ONE FROM A LITTER BORN AT OUR AUNT'S HOUSE.
MEOW

IT WAS A BIGGER COMPANY THAN I EXPECTED.
I can't believe how much blood they took.
SEN SAID...
...THAT IT'S MEDICINE THAT CURES PAIN.
H-HEY.
BUT WE MADE A LOT OF MONEY.
I was even offered a job.
AS A GUINEA PIG THAT CAN TALK...
HOLD ON, NIJUKU.
DID YOU GET HURT?
NO, NOT ME.
KURO-CHA! SEN!
NIJUKU!
You came all the way here on your own?
WHEN SANJU DOES WHAT SHE WANTS...
...SHE SQUEEZES TOO HARD. SO...
MEDICINE!
GIVE ME THE MEDICINE FROM YESTER-DAY!
HUH!?
...THE KITTY'S ARM...
...FELL OFF.

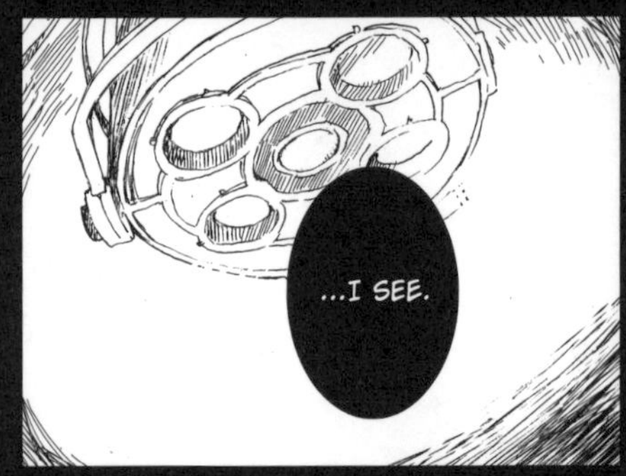
...I SEE.

Well, you know.
It was bound to happen.

EVEN THOUGH I'M WORRIED WHAT MIGHT COME OF IT...
...A LITTLE SENSE OF PAIN MIGHT BE NECES-SARY.
PAIN?

First, just lecture her on the difference...
...between breaking a flower stem and breaking a cat's leg.
IT'S GOING TO BE TOUGH TO TELL HER.

YOU'LL FEEL IT WHEN IT HURTS.
BY FEELING PAIN, YOUR BODY'S DEFENSES WILL ACTIVATE...
WHAT'S PAIN?

SO I SHOULD TALK ABOUT MORALS AND LECTURE HER ABOUT THE NOBILITY OF LIFE?
DON'T BE RIDICU-LOUS.

INSTINCT THAT WILL MAKE YOU REMEM-BER...
...NOT TO REPEAT THE SAME THING.

I CAN'T EVEN EXPLAIN TO THEM...
...HOW THEY CAME TO BE ALIVE.

SELCRAIG WAS A BRAVE MAN.
A STREET-WISE SAILOR.

CAN WE HOLD HANDS?
HUH? SURE.

HE RAN INTO A GHOST OF A WHALE ON HIS FIFTH VOYAGE.
SELCRAIG'S SHIP WAS DESTROYED, AND HE LOST HIS RIGHT LEG.

......
I'M SORRY.
WHY ARE YOU APOLOGIZING?

BUT HE CUT OPEN THE WHALE'S BELLY...
...AND MADE A PROSTHETIC USING WHALE BONE.

'COS YOU'RE MAD.
I'M NOT MAD.
YOUR VOICE IS THE ANGRY VOICE.
THE OWNER OF THE CAT IS MAD.

KURO-CHAN.
I CAME TO GET YOU.

BUT YOU'RE ACTING DIFFERENT.
AND YOUR HAND'S REALLY COLD.
....

SANJU.
LET'S HAVE A CHAT.

SANJU.
DO YOU KNOW WHY MY HAND IS COLD?

OH, I BROUGHT IT JUST IN CASE.
BUT YOU DON'T NEED THIS MEDICINE, RIGHT?
MEDI-CINE! NO!!

LOOK CARE-FULLY.
LOOK AT MY PINKY THAT YOU'RE SQUEEZING.
....

NOTHING HURTS.
AND NOTHING'S WRONG.
I SEE. BUT...

...THE COLOR'S CHANG-ING.
YEAH.
WITH NO BLOOD FLOWING, IT'S GOING TO TURN RED, AND THEN BLUE...

...I THINK I SHOULD ...
...GIVE YOU A LITTLE WOUND BEFORE IT'S TOO LATE.

...AND EVENTUALLY, THIS PINKY WILL STOP MOVING.

YOU DON'T CALL THIS HOLDING HANDS.
MY BLOOD AND YOUR FEELINGS ARE BLOCKED RIGHT HERE.
IF YOU CONTINUE TO DO THE SAME THING...
...I MIGHT EVEN LOSE MORE FINGERS.
AND THEN, WHEN WE REALLY CAN'T HOLD HANDS...
...MAYBE YOU'LL FINALLY UNDER-STAND.
BUT...
...IF MY HAND IS THE PRICE FOR YOUR UNDER-STANDING ...
...I'D GIVE IT GLADLY.
LET'S GO HOME.
NIJUKU'S WORRIED TOO.

And then?
Why are you so depressed?
WELL, UM...

WHACK

...IT'S DIFFI-CULT TO TEACH.
I DON'T KNOW IF I GAVE MEDICINE OR POISON.
Both would've been the same. It's about the end result.

Either way, it was necessary to Sanju now.
She won't have an answer right away. Let's give her time.

DON'T EVER COME BACK.
I'LL NEVER FORGIVE YOU.

But let me say this.
It's a myth that you can make up blood with tomato juice.
WHAT? REALLY?
!!!
BURP

WERE YOU ABLE TO TALK TO THEM?
YEAH.
WHAT DOES IT MEAN...
...TO NEVER FORGIVE?
WELL...
...EVEN IF THIS FADES FROM THEIR MEMORIES ...
...YOU SHOULDN'T FORGET.

Phew.
Setup complete.
Oh? Were you in charge of the fire today?
SANJU ASKED ME TO SWITCH.
Hmm.
AM I WEAK?
You're so weak.
She forced you to switch, right?
NO.
I'M FINE WHEN SANJU IS MAD.
BUT WHEN SANJU CRIES, I LOSE.
?
MY EARS AND TAIL...
...GET CRUSHED.
Aah.
You got a "wound"...
...from Kuro.
YOU JUST HAVE TO SAY SORRY.
NIJUKU!
LOOK, NIJUKU!
I'LL GIVE YOU THE BIGGEST ONE!

"I DON'T REMEMBER BUYING THESE CANS."

THANKS SO MUCH FOR JOINING US AGAIN FOR THE FOURTH VOLUME OF *SHOULDER-A-COFFIN KURO*.

SATOKO KIYUDUKI, 2013

"To us witches, these two swellings on our bosoms are proof that we can do anything."
(Free translation)
"Unfortunately, you don't appear to have that POTENTIAL."
SHARANRA
Those simply playing at witchcraft should return to Halloween Town to prepare for Christmas.
The witch who says, "Pirika?"
The witch who says, "Maralic?"

shoulder a coffin,

kuro

4

Presented by Satoko Kiyuduki

TRANSLATION NOTES

Page 104
In Japanese, the term for "white clover" is *shiroba* and the term for "four-leaf clover" is *yotsuba no kuroba*. As *kuro* also means "black," this is what Nikuju and Sanju repeat in the last panel, hence their confusion.

Page 122
Nijuku and Sanju's questions refer to the spells of famous anime witches. "The witch who says, 'Mahalic?'" is Sally, the titular character from *Sally the Witch*, one of the earliest magical girl anime series, while "The witch who says, 'Pirika?'" is *Ojamajo Doremi*'s protagonist, Doremi Harukaze.

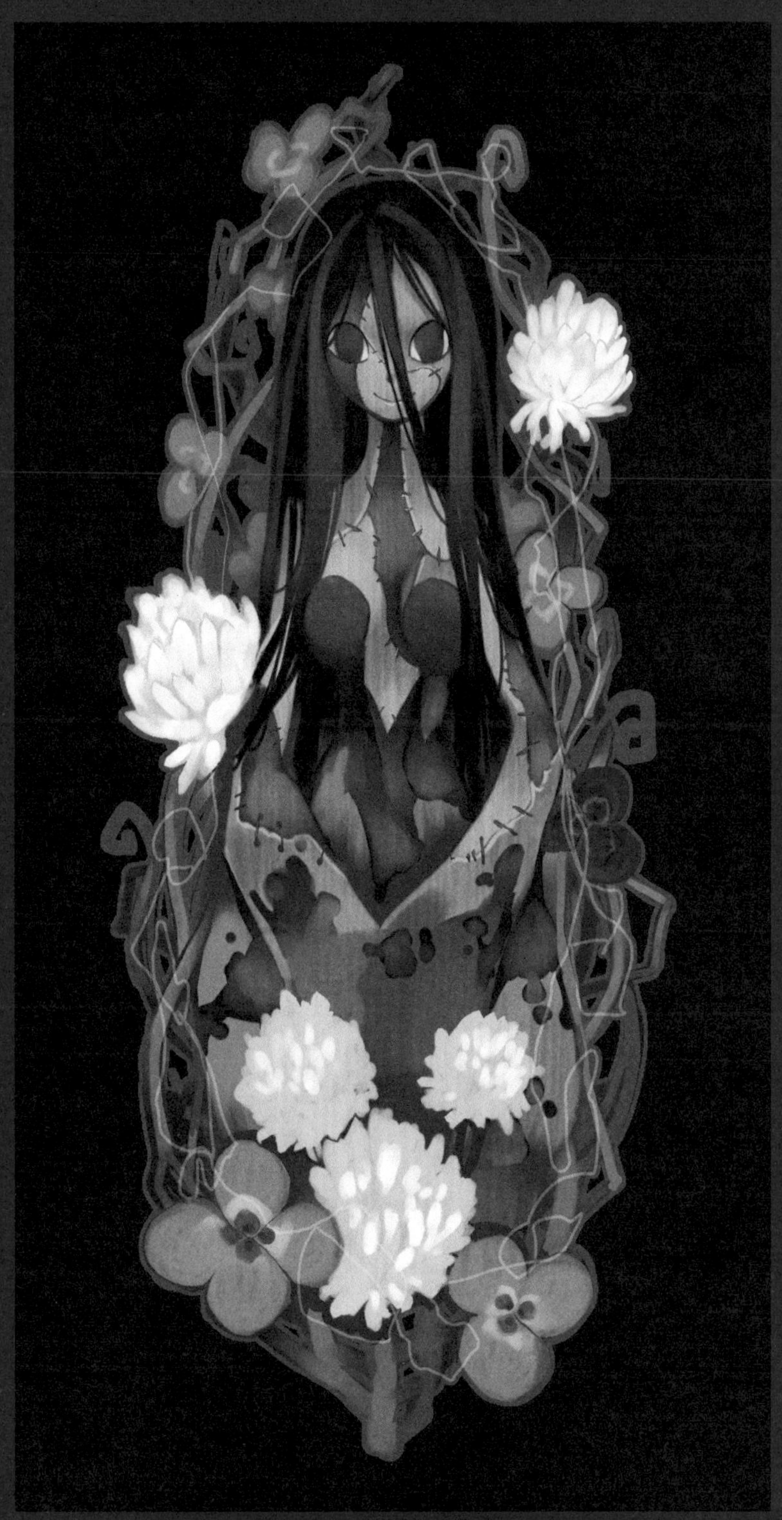

SHOULDER-A-COFFIN KURO 4

SATOKO KIYUDUKI

Translation: Satsuki Yamashita Lettering: Lys Blakeslee

Yen Press
Hachette Book Group
237 Park Avenue, New York, NY 10017

www.HachetteBookGroup.com
www.YenPress.com

Yen Press is an imprint of Hachette Book Group, Inc. The Yen Press name and logo are trademarks of Hachette Book Group, Inc.

First Yen Press Edition: September 2014

ISBN: 978-0-316-33588-1

10 9 8 7 6 5 4 3 2 1

RRD-C

Printed in the United States of America